DAWN
TILL DUSK

DAWN
TILL DUSK

RACING'S CHAMPIONS:
BEHIND THE SCENES

COLIN CAMERON

FOREWORD BY SIR PETER O'SULLEVAN

DEDICATION

To Emily

Published in 2005 by Highdown,
an imprint of Raceform Ltd
Compton, Newbury, Berkshire, RG20 6NL

Raceform Ltd is a wholly-owned subsidiary of Trinity Mirror plc

A CIP catalogue record for this book is available from the British Library.

ISBN 1-905156-12-X

Cover designed by Tracey Scarlett

Interiors designed by Fiona Pike

Printed and bound in Great Britain by William Clowes Ltd, Beccles, Suffolk

CONTENTS

ACKNOWLEDGEMENTS

A thank you to all the trainers and stable office staff who were instrumental in ensuring I was able to make contact with the eleven grooms and work riders who are the heart of this book, and the biggest thank you of all to each of them for their time and patience. Thank you to Betfair for part-funding the printing of this book in return for all royalties being routed to the charity, Racing Welfare. Thank you to the *Racing Post*'s Nick Godfrey for commissioning the series At The Sharp End that featured in the newspaper for three months at the beginning of 2004 and which was the inspiration for this book. Thank you also to Chris Smith, editor of the *Racing Post*, for supporting the series with handsome space every Sunday for three months. Thank you to Jonathan Taylor at Highdown – and also Brough Scott – for seeing the potential to widen the reach and range of the subject of stable staff into a book that at the very least will generate money for a worthwhile charity. Thank you also to Richard Lowther and Ashley Rumney, colleagues at Raceform who have ensured that any mistakes in the text are alone the fault of the author, to Tracey Scarlett for her excellence in creating a cover worthy of the subject matter, and to Julian Brown for nursing the project home. Thank you, too, to Sir Peter O'Sullevan for honouring and enhancing the final text with a foreword. Further thanks to Betfair's Mark Davies, for decisively supporting this project, regardless of what time differences he was facing, and to Alan Byrne for supplying his hallmark mix of carrot and stick to encourage this book's completion. Thanks to the British Horseracing Board's Kate Walthew for supplying images by Arnhel de Serra and thanks to him for their inclusion. Thanks to Betfair's Antonia Sharpe and Georgina Hard for their combined efforts to promote the cause, and to The Jockey Club's John Maxse for his work on behalf of Racing Welfare. And thank you to all the partners of those featured in this book for the kind hospitality offered to me during my intrusions. Chocolate biscuits were more than I deserved.

FOREWORD

For three centuries, give or take a decade or so, the sport of horse racing has been in a state of reasonably affluent crisis. Throughout the period there have been two constants: the horses and the workforce. Other contributors to the maintenance of the Thoroughbred in all his glory are entitled to claim crucial status. And they do. But it is the relationship between lad or lass and 'their' horse which is the heartbeat of a great, and oft misinterpreted, sport.

Colin Cameron not only highlights this mutual bond which develops between horse and partner (like Joyce Wallsgrove and Moonax) but reflects divergent aspects of training, the background to the preparation of some high profile performers and the personnel's views of their owners. In the latter category Lisa Jackson – longtime brilliant head girl at Philip Hobbs' – is quoted apropos multi-horsepowered Irishman J.P. McManus: "J.P. loves his horses and is genuinely concerned about how they all are. His horses all go back to his place in Ireland over the summer. They are completely checked out by the vets there for any damage or problems. They are turned out in a lovely environment. Obviously he has a lot of money. But even so, not many owners would incur the cost of flying all their horses home for a summer break."

Infinitely less happy with the post-racing treatment of National winner Hello Dandy was Greystoke lad Larry Poland. 'What happened to Dandy, roughed out in a field in the winter with no hay shouldn't be allowed,' he insisted before praising the 1984 hero's merciful rescue by pioneer Carrie Humble's wonderful Thoroughbred Rehabilitation Centre.

Much equine – and human – life is here. Dawn till dusk.

Sir Peter O'Sullevan
London

INTRODUCTION

British stable staff show a dedication that puts the efforts of many in much safer, significantly better paid jobs to shame. They also make a lot less noise in the process. This is a group for whom attention seeking is inversely related to hours worked.

This book is an effort to rectify that staff in Britain are rarely heard by the wider audience to the extent that their contribution to racing's greatest days warrants. Instead of carrying the often well-aired views of owners, trainers and jockeys, who have, respectively, underwritten, conditioned and ridden the sport's best known champions, these pages contain the thoughts and recollections of the men and women with even closer associations. Considering how involved a groom is with the horses in his or her care, opportunities to share at any decent sort of length their part in the fulfilment of potential have been limited. This book is hopefully something of a chance.

Most who follow racing have a Lester Piggott story. If you enjoy listening to them as much as telling your own then you should greatly enjoy the variations on this theme contained herein. If you don't have a Piggott story, you will by the time you have finished these pages. If you enjoy a good racing debate, you will find plenty of views to contest here. Dennis Wright partnered Shirley Heights on the gallops, the year before he won the Derby. Rodney Boult took over the saddle for the following season. They still beg to differ about aspects of their shared ride. Stuart Messenger and Jimmy Scott at least both concur that Shergar bolting ahead of the Derby in 1981 was far from ideal. Racing, along with every sport, is indeed about opinions like those of Boult, Wright, Messenger and Scott. This book is full of them.

For me, listening to the thoughts and recollections now contained in this book was an education. If I thought I had some grasp of horseracing before I started gathering the anecdotes and insights that make up this text, I was under no illusions on finishing that a complete understanding of horsemanship and stable craft will probably always be beyond me, not least because that would require a great deal more hard work than is usually scheduled. You may be better placed to argue over racing's finer points and well used to long hours in all weathers. Even if you disagree from a more credible position than your armchair with any thoughts expressed, you cannot begin to dispute that those expressing them are fully entitled to be heard. They know. They were there.

Royalties from this book will go to Racing Welfare to help fund the charity's excellent work. This is a worthy cause. As for the case for increasing the levels of stable staff pay, the argument for that is now so old you might begin to wonder whether anything substantial will ever be done to ensure that the general rewards for what is both skilled and dangerous labour truly reflect the nature of the work. If the argument for fairer pay needs strengthening further, this book, at a minimum, should convey what an essential role stable staff play in sustaining standards in British racing. Without whom is, I think, the relevant phrase.

Forgive any apparent lapses in memory. They are, most likely, my fault in failing to transcribe or recall accurately the thoughts this gifted group shared with me for what is really their book. Even if time has played tricks with the mind - in some cases we've gone back over 50 years - those interviewed nevertheless tell some grand old yarns. Whatever issue you take with their accounts, on this occasion give them the floor with good grace. They have earned it. You never know, your own recollections might well have become confused with the passage of time. To be sure, you really needed to have been there, from first light at dawn, until dusk.

Colin Cameron
September 2005

CHAPTER ONE
JOHN JOYCE

From Connaught to the present day

John Joyce has been in racing for five decades. For nearly all this time his name's been Jumbo. There are plenty of explanations for this billing, but the real one, according to the man himself, is this: at Tommy Shedden's Wetherby yard – Joyce's point of departure into the world of racing as an apprentice – Larry Major reckoned he was the image of Jumbo Wilkinson in the saddle. It's quite a compliment. Wilkinson and Major, who was a mainstay at Shedden's yard, were weighing-room princes of their day. The comparison has helped Joyce during the most testing of times since the not-so swinging sixties with Shedden.

A major black spot was a horror fall on the Newmarket gallops that left him requiring reconstructive surgery. Today, Joyce's left foot hasn't much of a heel to speak of. Strike action, now over 30 years ago, was also painful – to the pocket. Through simple excellence in horsemanship he has survived season after season. Newmarket's gallops remain his chosen place of work. But he has yet to make sense of the game's economics.

The alternative to Shedden's was Yorkshire's mines. Joyce's father worked underground, but he was determined that his son wouldn't suffer the same fate. Football had been a possibility, though a frame that amounted to less than seven stone hindered a natural talent for the sport. After trials at Huddersfield Town, Bill Shankly, who was the club manager in the late 1950s, told Joyce to become a jockey instead. At the same time Shankly told Denis Law to find some contact lenses, Joyce recalls.

Either apprenticeship would have been hard for Joyce. At the time, racing's deal for the next generation was akin to five years' slave labour. You signed, and the boss decided the drill. At Shedden's it was punishing – long hours in return for five shillings a week. Joyce galvanised the seven apprentices and took up their collective case for a rise. Establishing a mini union cost him any chance of rides in public. 'Tommy said I was a rebel, and he was probably right,' Joyce says. 'He reckoned I'd have the weighing room out too.' Plenty of trainers have since had to contest with Joyce's beliefs in what is right and wrong.

Initially he could stomach only two years of Shedden's first-up, best-dressed regime and basic diet of bread and jam. Then a chance meeting with an old colleague saved Joyce from permanently slipping out of racing altogether. He was spotted digging ditches by a fellow Shedden alumnus who had moved on to Jimmy Thompson's local yard. Once their former boss had been persuaded by an apology – through gritted teeth – to release Joyce's indentures, he was able to turn his back on manual labour and return to skilled work in the saddle.

In 1969 Joyce joined the workforce at Sir Noel Murless's yard. After Murless came a spell with Frank Cundell. Joyce then headed back to Wetherby for the rest of the 1970s, at Jack Hanson's yard. Then he took to the road again, back to Newmarket and Paul Kelleway, and onwards and upwards from there to join forces with the then plain Michael Stoute (thanks to Cliff Lines, who played Cupid). Joyce's next move, to Henry Cecil's operation, was a return of sorts to the Murless fold: at the time, Sir Noel's daughter Julie was Cecil's wife. Since then he has had spells with John Gosden (when he was still Newmarket-based), Jack Banks, Dave Morris, Stoute again, Bill O'Gorman (while the trainer's daughter Emma farmed the all-weather), Duncan Sasse (a true racing gent, Joyce maintains), William Haggas for three seasons, and, today, Pat Gilligan. The latter snapped up Joyce from under the nose of Ed Dunlop.

His perseverance with Newmarket and the town's ways doesn't indicate unconditional acceptance, though. 'I'll tell you what the place is really like,' he says with a big grin. 'A man stands on the edge of a cliff, looking very unhappy. A stranger stops to ask if he can help. "See those ships on the sea?" the man says. "I helped build over a hundred of them. No one remembers that. See those houses? Must have helped design nearly two hundred. No one remembers any of that. But just the one sheep – no one is ever going to forget!"' The redeeming factor was the town's depth in quality racehorses. For Joyce, Connaught, stabled at Sir Noel Murless's yard, was the first superstar. With Henry Cecil there was a trio of Derby winners in Slip Anchor, Reference Point and Old Vic, and the Classic-winning fillies Oh So Sharp, Diminuendo and Indian Skimmer. At Royal Ascot in 1987, a highly profitable seven winners.

Lester Piggott, like Joyce still a fixture in the town, remains a good friend. Steve Cauthen, who rode five of the Ascot winners of 1987, is another with whom Joyce has shared quality mornings. The American was perfect for winning Derbies in the front-running style that brought the best out of Slip Anchor, Reference Point and, in France, Old Vic. 'Steve was a great fellow,' says Joyce. 'Around the yard, when the time was right, he could have a real laugh. For front running, he was the perfect jockey. There was paint on his boots from when he won the Derby on Slip Anchor, hugging the rail. Actually, Henry didn't like horses running from the front. We sat down one day and I took the chance to see if he'd be persuaded. "Just let's say that they don't mind being in front," I said. Now a mile-and-a-half horse jumps off first travelling at, say, 35mph – steady compared to a top sprinter who can manage over 40. Now imagine that the horse maintains that, and he is a comfortable six to eight lengths ahead. Ask yourself this: if he was a car, how fast would you have to go to reach him, let alone overtake? "Does it work like that with horses?" Henry asked me! An all-right guy, Henry. Must have sacked me a good few times but he knew which side his bread was buttered. Always took me back in the end.'

Slip Anchor benefited directly. 'I rode Slip Anchor on the gallops and straight away got on with him,' Joyce recalls. 'Paddy Rudkin, Henry Cecil's key man at the time, could see that for sure, and I certainly did my very best to make sure it looked that way. At Henry's, there was a furlong-round gallop. You would canter, then walk a few steps, then trot a few, then walk again. Except Slip Anchor wouldn't always trot. He'd kick out and be a right pain. So I at least made sure that Slip Anchor behaved for the stretch that Paddy and Henry could see. Then, when we were out of view again, he'd be back at it, pratting around for me, just like he did for anyone else. Henry and Paddy were never the wiser. I wasn't going to give up Slip Anchor. I always knew that he was good. In the end, we got on just fine.'

Of the three Henry Cecil horses – Slip Anchor, Reference Point and Old Vic – Joyce was most instrumental with the first-named. En route to Epsom in 1985, he helped the colt overcome breathing problems that left his brain starved of oxygen after exercise. 'He did have real problems on the gallops. At the end of work he'd stagger around, spinning, whoever was in the saddle. At the races, too. Lester rode him once and he spun afterwards that day for him, too. Lester said to Henry, "Keep him away from me, he's dangerous." The vets said the problem was that at times oxygen didn't always get through to his brain. My idea was, after a strong canter, instead of pulling him up after a few strides, which would be normal, I'd look to jog him around a bit. "Like in athletics," I said to Henry, "when the winner goes on a lap of honour in the Olympics to celebrate." Henry agreed. It was worth a go. The next time, I trotted him round in big circles while his breathing settled down. After that, he never spun with me.

'We'd take a canister of oxygen to the race and give him a blast if he looked like he needed it. We had one at Lingfield for the Derby Trial, which Slip Anchor won so comfortably. On that occasion, instead of giving him a blast up the nostrils when he had finished, Steve Cauthen made sure that Slip Anchor did his circles after the race to get him straight. In the race, he absolutely bolted in. Lester rode in the race, couldn't get near Slip Anchor. I said to him afterwards, "Does that win the Derby?" "Take f***ing catching," he shouted back. I was already thinking about Epsom. After that trial we knew he was up to winning the big one, and I made sure, as best I could, on the gallops that we kept enough in reserve for the day.

'Once we had sorted out the breathing there was only one significant scare. We had a lucky escape just two weeks before the race. It was a strong, uphill canter. My reins had these clips, rather than the old-fashioned buckles, and the clip had sheared off (Henry did away with them after this). I was left holding with just one hand and I couldn't pull on that as everything, the bridle included, would just have come off. It could have been the end for both of us if he had

been galloping blind. I put a loop in the rein I had and with
my other hand slipped two fingers into Slip Anchor's neck
strap. Then I just flicked his throat lash, which dropped
down, and that slowed him down. There was a wall ahead
at the top of the gallop. That at least worked to help him
stop. What really made him pull up was that we had done
the gallop many, many times. He knew the routine, and
when it was time to stop. Then, like I had taught him, he
trotted round in his big circles, which had become part of
his normal routine. When his breathing had settled down, I
finally got off him.'

Reference Point followed, and then along came Old Vic.
They met Joyce's standards for colts set by Connaught,
winner of the Prince of Wales Stakes twice and an Eclipse.
'Reference Point as a yearling looked like a big carthorse,'
Joyce says. 'He was huge. Even walking he could hardly
get out his own way. Nobody rated him much, but I got on
him for a gallop. There wasn't much speed then, but he had
real power. You could feel that all right. Afterwards I said to
Frank Storey, who was another one of the key men at
Warren Place, "This one just needs a kick up the backside to
get him fit." He was so laid back and would trip up four
times before he made it to the gallops. Frank rode him after
that and really sorted him out. When he was awake you'd
see him stride out all right. At other times he was so placid
and laid back.'

Reference Point's problems were at least as serious as
Slip Anchor's. 'Reference Point had a much tougher time,

all considered, over the winter,' says Joyce. 'The issue was mainly his sinuses. In the end, they drilled a hole in his head for it. It wasn't that long to go before the 1987 Derby and vets, owners, Henry, they all had a big decision to make. He had not been a Guineas type, but he was a real Derby horse, so they went for the operation in the hope that it would make the difference. They drilled the hole and all this stuff – snot, basically – came out. Every day more and more. We'd have to clean him up every time he exercised. The miracle was that, with the Derby in mind, there wasn't much of an interruption to his programme. He was back on the gallops pretty quickly after the operation, and that meant he stayed on course for Epsom.

'Old Vic was much more straightforward. I think that is actually what I remember most, looking back. He was pretty placid and could be a bit sluggish, but that can be what the big ones like him are like – the Reference Points and the Old Vics of this world. But they don't seem to get tendons and joints, the sort of niggling injury that can sideline them, on and off. It is because they are not as active. As a four-year-old Slip Anchor was so active. He flipped over in his box once and did his leg in, also a joint. Of course, horses like Old Vic do need plenty of work. Bonhomie, who won the King Edward VII Stakes at Ascot in 1986, was another big, gross horse. You really needed plenty of work to get the best from them. If you let them get over-big they have too much weight on their joints. But if you can avoid that happening, they don't seem to pick up injuries like some of the others.

'The first time Old Vic ran, in September 1988, I knew he was good. That year Michael Stoute saddled what looked like a real talent – Icona, a bit of a tearaway. He won his maiden by about six lengths. When they met at the racecourse in April 1989 Old Vic beat him by ten lengths, and it could have been fifteen lengths. Icona ended up winning the Magnet Cup at 12–1. Old Vic was only moderate as a two-year-old, but the improvement he showed over the winter meant he developed into a really serious three-year-old. At two, the lad who looked after him asked me after I rode the horse whether he would turn out to be special. I had to be honest. "Wouldn't say so," I said. But as a three-year-old? A different story. He was always a big, fine animal and he showed some form. But something changed with him during the winter. He became a different horse. We saw that for sure when he won the French Derby at Chantilly in 1989. Hard to put my finger on why or when the change took place. I saw him day after day. That can mean you don't notice improvements. You have to go away for a bit on holiday and then come back. Then you see the ones who have done well – he's grown, like the look of him, he's come on.'

In the end, a Derby for each colt. 'I didn't actually go to Slip Anchor's Derby,' Joyce continues. 'I watched the race in the pub with some other lads and the boys from Stoute's yard. They had Shadeed, the 2,000 Guineas winner, running. We ordered six bottles of champagne before the start and agreed with the barman that we'd pay if we won and Stoutey's lot would if they did. At Tattenham Corner, I said, "Open them up now, would you?" We sprayed it around like we'd won the Grand Prix.

'He was so laid back at Henry's. He became a runaway at four. We had a gallop for him, and this time Steve Cauthen rode. Afterwards, Henry asked Steve what he thought. "This horse ain't worth a kick in the ass," he said. In the end, a real disappointment as a four-year-old. Probably bottomed him, winning the Derby. He was certainly worked hard before the race. But there's nothing wrong with that if they peak on the day, and he certainly did.

'I heard that Reference Point turned into a savage at stud. Old Vic? I saw him again when I was loading up horses for the BBA [British Bloodstock Agency] one time and he was on the flight. He had been retired to stud by then. I asked, for old times' sake, if I could load him. Just to see him. He had a neck as thick as a garden wall and a backside the size of my kitchen. I also went to see Slip Anchor at Plantation Stud a couple of times. I asked the groom there if I could go into his box. I was told you are not supposed to. Then I explained who I was – "OK then." I blew up his nose and he made a noise. I asked if he did that with everyone. "He can smell the Guinness," the lad said.'

*

The economics of working in racing has often required of Joyce the best of his inherited sense of humour. When he was trying to break free from Tommy Shedden, 'who was hanging on to my indentures', he and his father went to see a solicitor. 'The solicitor asked, "Do you have any money?" "We've a million quid," said my father. "Are you joking?" the solicitor asked. "You started it," said father.'

Things were a little better in Newmarket. 'For my part in Connaught's gallops, Jim Joel, his owner, gave me £500. He never spoke to me, or anything like that. He'd come round and look at his horses. One day he gave me an envelope. I had to wait until he'd gone round the corner to open it. A lot of money in those days, that's for sure. I got the same after Slip Anchor's Derby. I think Lord Howard de Walden, who owned the colt, had dug up 50 tenners from his garden! I was expecting a bit more, but a drink is a drink. Then, a few days later, Paddy Rudkin went down to the off-licence and came back with a few beers. It isn't every day you win the Derby. After that we piled down to the pub and carried on. There were also a few glasses at the owner's Plantation Stud, but he did run out of champagne.

'At Henry's, the real mystery for me was the logic to do with Water Cay. He was one of my favourites, and the owner, Peter Burrell, was a smashing man. Would always give me £100 if he won any sort of race, just for passing the winning post. Even when we won something at odds like 7–1 on I'd still get the usual. Except for finishing second at Royal Ascot in 1987 to Then Again. For that, nothing, even though Mr Burrell won about £30,000. Smashing bloke, as I said, but I couldn't ever work that out.'

Come the early 1970s, enough was enough. 'The first

strike about general pay in Newmarket was unofficial, ahead of the dispute in 1975,' Joyce recalls. 'We met at the Con Club in Newmarket to discuss what we were going to do. I said, "Go to work in the morning, muck out and give them water, but don't exercise them or go racing. Then, at evening stables, if they will have you, muck out again and bed them down. In other words, look after the horses." Instead, people said, "All-out strike!" In the end I stayed out for three days. On the second day I was on the gallops and saw students – I don't know where they were from – burying bottles in the ground. I knew then that I didn't want to be associated with the strike any more.' Such sabotage was too much for a true horseman. 'I went back to Sir Noel Murless's yard, where I was working. I told the boss that I went on strike to support the boys but after what I had seen I didn't want any part of it. He said, "You are stupid. You are doing something to get them another five bob a week and I am paying you more than that already. Get on with your work." But it was different after that. Just never right.'

*

The Christmas party for Henry Cecil's yard usually took place in the New Year, and it was often fancy dress. Henry and his then wife, Julie, came one year as flamenco dancers, while Joyce turned up as a clown (therefore free to have some fun). The Cecil mix of instinct and eccentricity worked, especially with fillies. 'Henry was brilliant with them,' Joyce says. 'He would not overdo it with them. It was instinct. You cannot put your finger on it. Henry was brilliant with fillies because . . . you cannot say the word. He just was.

'Oh So Sharp was like a colt. We used to say she had colt's genes in her. She would strike out and rear up just like a colt, and if you saw her pratting about you would never think that she was a filly. Henry got inside her head. Diminuendo was more feminine, smaller, more petite than Oh So Sharp. But she didn't have the same speed. Who did? And she was a right cow. She just wouldn't go anywhere. Henry got the best out of her too. Indian Skimmer was the same as Diminuendo – worse maybe. She just wouldn't go on to the gallops. She turned that way in time. I think she just thought, "I've had enough of this." With fillies as good as her, they can be really hyper. It is a fine line between that and going nuts.'

Oh So Sharp was the queen, the benchmark for fillies, the very best of Newmarket. 'They tried her with a girl to see if that might calm her down but she was always a handful – on the gallops, in the paddock, wherever,' Joyce continues. 'She was always performing. She knew right from the start that she was a natural. Watching her, despite all her antics, you couldn't miss it. She was a superstar, and she knew it.' Diminuendo brought her attitude three years later. 'If you were on your way to the gallops, she would stop at a fence and rub herself just to try and get you off her. I gave her a lead a few times but it was hard work. Instead of up the gallops, she would go off into the woods. We'd all have to go after her, but she wouldn't budge – a real madam. Indian Skimmer was the same. But on the racecourse, and on the gallops when we finally got her going on them, she wouldn't put a foot wrong. It was just getting her there, and started.

'You could not get to the bottom of Oh So Sharp. The first serious gallop I saw was with this other filly who I think had broken the track record over seven furlongs at Newmarket – Fatah Flare. In the gallop, she wiped the floor with her. Then she went from April right through the summer of 1985 to the St Leger. She won a third Classic at Doncaster, even though there were those in the yard who reckoned she had lost a bit of her sparkle. Pure class got her through. What an animal, especially when you consider all the performing and antics at home between her races. She would have been unbeaten if Petoski had not got his head in front in the King George. Since then Steve Cauthen has said that it was his fault that she was beaten in the race. I remember on the morning of the race, I said to him, "The only way you'll get beaten in this race today is if they gang up on you." And they did. If you watch the race, they quickened three times. They jumped off and quickened, then quickened in running, and then again at the end of the race. That certainly got to the bottom of the winner, Petoski. Back at the yard, no one really said anything. Oh So Sharp's reputation hardly suffered as a result. What's the point of cheering only when they win? Steve certainly never blamed anyone else. He was bigger than that.

'The pity was that she went out of training at the end of her three-year-old days. At stud she never looked great, and she died fairly young. They reckon she was never very happy away from the yard. There was no one to perform to, or show off to. And she didn't breed anything very special. At four, she would have been unbeatable. Everything was right for a horse like that to have another year.

'Diminuendo was really lucky to be racing at all for the time she did. There was a big storm in 1987, which wrecked Newmarket. Diminuendo was fortunate to escape in one piece from that. A lad called Nobby, who lived in the yard and is sadly dead now, looked after her. The night the wind was up and the trees were rattling Nobby got up and moved her from her box, which was off the main yard, to what he thought would be a safer place along with the rest of the fillies. For the rest of the night the storm continued to rage, and one of the trees brought down cut her box in half. In the morning we had to set horses free that were blocked in their stables. There were plenty of loose ones too. For a while, part of the yard was completely out of action.'

It was Indian Skimmer who provided the patriotic pride. 'She went to France in 1987 and beat Miesque,' Joyce recalls. 'The weekend papers were full of it, being us versus the French, and it was great to beat them. It always is. The day reminded me of a fellow called Norman. I'd worked with him at Stoutey's. Before I arrived, he looked after a filly called Fair Salinia. She won the Oaks with a French filly behind her. Apparently, that day in the winner's enclosure the Queen came up to him, patted him on the shoulder and said, "Well done, young man. I am glad we beat those French." "Well, we did at Waterloo and all, didn't we?" Norman replied.'

*

At William Haggas's yard, Lester Piggott always wanted to work with Joyce. 'Lester would ride out for his son-in-law,' Joyce recalls, 'but the lads didn't appreciate him. He didn't mix with them and there was no chat. That was because they had nothing to say to him and he had nothing to say to them. We'd be in in the morning, waiting for our orders. Willie Haggas would ask Lester, "Could you go up there and work three furlongs? Now, who do you want with you?" He'd always say, "Send Jumbo." I'd ask him proper questions and he'd give me proper answers. The reason he could be difficult with some people is that he could never be bothered to listen and work out what they were asking.

'That was hard with Norman, who had talked to the Queen after Fair Salinia's Oaks win. He had a bit of a speech impediment. Back at Henry's one day, we had a spare at Leicester so Norman was asked to lead up a filly for us. Lester was riding and he didn't know Norman or the horse. After Lester got a leg up he asked Norman if the filly was any good. "I don't know – not mine," said Norman, sounding just like Lester. Lester thought he was mimicking him. "You can f**k off," he said, and hit him on the head with his stick. Afterwards, Norman was waiting to catch the filly and lead her in but Lester went straight past him to Henry in the unsaddling enclosure. "I don't want anything to do with that bloke," he said. "He's taking the piss." Henry tried to explain. "He talks like that too."

'Have a proper conversation with Lester, and he'll listen. With Lester, the first thing you say is important. If you say something stupid he won't hear you after that. I asked him about his son, Jamie. Lester's goal is to see him ride a winner. Sadly, his son is no more interested in horses than the man on the moon. A biggish lad, too. You'd think your heart and soul would be in racing with Lester as your dad. But with him, absolutely nothing, not a spark. No rhyme or reason to that. Would be tough to be a jockey and Lester's son, mind.'

Piggott admired Sir Ivor above all – quite a compliment to Connaught, second to the colt in the Epsom Derby of 1968. 'I discussed with Lester whether stamina beat Connaught at Epsom,' Joyce recalls, 'on the basis that if you take Sir Ivor out of the equation, Connaught wins the Derby very easily. Lester's take? I once asked him, straight up, which was the best horse he had ever ridden. "Telling you straight, the best was Sir Ivor," he said. "Some machine . . ."'

Joyce's part in preparing Connaught at four at Sir Noel Murless's yard was his first brush with greatness. 'At Sir Noel Murless's you never cut any corners. Everything had to be done properly. For me it wasn't so much as going from Doncaster Rovers to the Premier League; more like going from Coronation Street to Dallas. Sir Noel and Lady Murless were smashing people, very down to earth. Lady Murless bought me a moped to help me get to and from the yard in the mornings. The guv'nor always called me Joyce. Not, I think, because he was a snob; more because there were enough Johns around to confuse him.

'At four, Connaught was kept to ten furlongs by the guv'nor. He won the Prince of Wales Stakes at Royal Ascot two years in a row, 1969 and 1970. In 1970 he also won the Eclipse. He'd sometimes fall out of the stalls and still win. Once Sandy Barclay nearly fell off but someone gave him a hand up and the pair of them went on to win. On the gallops, I'd set off in front racecourse side – me, Connaught and three others. I'd lead off and Connaught would be plumb last. They'd hold Connaught for as long as possible – sometimes just three furlongs. We'd go at such a clip but he'd still come through. Even horses like Welsh Pageant, a champion miler, couldn't go with him.

'Connaught could play up a bit at the start by the time he was four. By the season after his Derby run he'd become a big bulk of a horse. That was really the problem. The stalls in those days were smaller. They have since made them wider and longer. With the old design, to get him in the stalls and keep him settled – well, he'd freak. He was also a colt – pretty cocky, a real Jack the Lad. I mean, walking round Side Hill in Newmarket he ripped the sheet straight off the horse in front of him. He was busy thinking about other things. A real colt. When you fed him you had to tie him up or he would have you.'

Teaming up with Cecil and rejoining the Murless fold in January 1985, with a Derby just months away, gave Joyce the most productive racing years of his career. 'We had the best staff in the world: lads who knew what they were talking about and could ride anything, the best trainer in the world, the best horses, and the best jockey – Steve Cauthen, with a clock in his head. When we weren't on the road we watched the racing down at the pub with the bookies handy. For Royal Ascot in 1987 – seven winners. We finished the week with money coming out of our ears. Midyan won the Jersey Stakes at 11–2. I started off by having £100 on him. The others were at all prices, and Ascot prices at that. In a season with Henry you'd back some losers, of course, but not many. You might pick a couple, but there would be three winners. And then there would be weeks like at Ascot in 1987.

'The peak that year was Paean. He won the Gold Cup, which capped everything. He was a big, gangly type, long legs and, to sit on, a great stride. You can tell the difference between the stayers and the sprinters. He was a long strider who was always going to make up into a great galloper. Like Slip Anchor. With them, you wanted to make the running. They have speed, too. I learnt that when I was asked to help prepare one trained by Michael Stoute for the Ascot Gold Cup. We went over racecourse side with him. I knew he was a Cup horse, all right. Stoutey said, "Jump off five furlongs with these two-year-olds. Just go at a nice clip." Now, consider that I'm riding a two-mile-plus horse, so I get him going as I am up against five-furlong two-year-olds. After a furlong I look round. They aren't near me. I keep going further and further ahead. Stoutey comes up. "What's going on?" he asks. Stoutey was pretty cross, I can tell you. I had to explain. He may be a stayer, but they can have speed.'

At the other end of racing's scale to Piggott, Murless, Stoute and Cecil, stored away in Joyce's mind are memories of Amber Valley at Jack Hanson's yard. 'As a colt, he wouldn't have it,' Joyce says. 'We all told Jack Hanson to pick his pockets, so Jack had him gelded. After that he started to win races. Before, he just wanted to do what colts want to do rather than get on with his job. After he hit double figures Jack said, "Fancy getting that horse cut." But if we hadn't he wouldn't have won anything. He wouldn't have been Amber Valley. As he got older, he got clever, but if you told him what to do he'd do it for you.'

Garden Society is the 2005 season's great cause. 'James Toller had him as a three-year-old. He was an OK horse, then he sustained an injury. The vets thought he would never run again. So they gave him away to a lad called Yorkie, who lives in Newmarket. He nursed him, then brought him back into training at the O'Gorman yard, where Bill and his son PJ are based. Then, to give him a change of scenery, we got him. When he arrived at Pat Gilligan's his back was all out. Once we sorted that out, he started winning again. With his back fine, he flew. He was only off a nothing handicap mark, so we took him to Wolverhampton where he won like he did, at odds of 16–1.

That was a Saturday. We were back on the Monday and he won again, this time at 5–2. A couple more runs under his belt after that we tried him over two miles. This time, a winner at 10–1.' Next time out, he was beaten a head. 'His back's not perfect. But when it's right, we'll win a nice handicap with him.'

CHAPTER TWO
JOYCE WALLSGROVE

From Early Spring to Maids Causeway

Joyce Wallsgrove likes science fiction films. For her, they are pure escapism. Not that she has needed much. For over 30 years, the game has sustained an appeal more than enduring enough for her to remain a part of Planet Racing. From employment with Bob Turnell and then his son Andy, to her post as manager of Newmarket's racecourse stables, she has rarely considered leaving the world of thoroughbreds.

Before Wallsgrove arrived at headquarters and the yard that serves the town's Rowley Mile and July Course, there was the best part of two decades with Barry Hills, seven of those years as head girl. She signed off in 2004 by preparing the mighty Maids Causeway for the 1,000 Guineas at Newmarket the following year, where she finished second before success at York in Royal Ascot's Coronation Stakes. Her time at Hills' included spells at the trainer's South Bank stables, and before that at Manton. At the latter she also spent eighteen months with Michael Dickinson before Hills was drafted in by the estate's owner, Robert Sangster. The contrast in style with the old-school approach of Turnell senior, where it all started for her, remains striking.

When she was a teenager, boys were almost as interesting as any horse nuance, she observes with a smile that says there was never really a contest. After riding-school lessons shared with friends, she stayed with the more intelligent breed while the pack chased after the weaker sex. Married, eighteen, and in temporary exile up Lanark way, in Scotland, she rode point-to-points and broke horses around wasted hours working in a shop. The chance to make her passion a full-time pursuit came in 1974 when Bob Turnell advertised a job back down south that came with a cottage attached to his yard. As well as the chance to ride the likes of Early Spring, the two-mile king of his day, Turnell also gave Wallsgrove confidence. It was still hard though, as she admits. There weren't many girls in racing back then. At Turnell's the ratio was about five to one; today, some yards are near enough 50–50. Headscarves were mandatory. 'You had to prove yourself, that you could do the job as well as a lad,' Wallsgrove explains. 'You had to be one of them.'

Andy Turnell ultimately took over from his father, which meant a shift to the Flat for Wallsgrove. Then Michael Dickinson called in person, so she said farewell to Turnell junior's Maori Venture after just one season, ahead of the Jim Joel gelding's success in the Grand National of 1987. Manton in 1985 was an irresistible adventure waiting to happen. A bonny filly called Snowkist made it hard for Wallsgrove to turn her back on the place when Barry Hills replaced Dickinson. Hills himself relocated back to his old South Bank base at the beginning of the new decade. Wallsgrove moved with him. This time she couldn't abandon Bold Russian. The colt supplied some much-needed continuity between the two yards and capped his rewarding career in 1991 with a Celebration Mile at Goodwood.

Blues Traveller came after Bold Russian, in 1993. The colt took her into the frame at Epsom, then popped up again when Wallsgrove was visiting New Zealand. Classic-wise, Blues Traveller was a forerunner to Moonax. Wallsgrove was one of the few who had Moonax's measure, and in 1994 the partnership yielded a St Leger and Group One success in France. The colt remains the only horse to win both the French and English St Legers. Mornings spent looking after Rainbow High, and afternoons winning the Chester Cup, were the reward for the patience Wallsgrove showed in nurturing one of racing's more, shall we agree, unpredictable performers.

Along the way, the company has been good. 'With the jumpers, who ran and ran for years, there was a camaraderie,' Wallsgrove recalls. In mind, as well as Early Spring, are Birds Nest and Beacon Light, who both schooled thrillingly over hurdles. 'The same horses would meet at the track winter after winter and you'd get to know the other lads. Racing was like a reunion.' In the Flat game, she encountered a curious, young Peter Chapple-Hyam, assisting Barry Hills at Manton. Others, such as Sangster, all the Hills family including Barry's wife Penny and the twin jockeys Richard and Michael, and Darryll Holland back at South Bank combined to make sometimes long stable hours pass swiftly.

In her new role at Newmarket, Wallsgrove still draws on plenty of the tricks she has learnt over the years in the front line. Don't wear perfume around the colts, for example; then they're less of a handful around the fillies. For this general grounding, which continues to serve her into a fourth racing decade, credit begins with the late Bob Turnell. 'Bob was brilliant,' Wallsgrove says. 'He'd never ask you to do anything he didn't think you could do. A kind man as well. While I was there with him both my parents died. He said, "Take as much time as you need."' A great man, Bob, she insists. 'I owe him everything. He said to me, "It doesn't matter what you look like in the saddle, you have got the hands. That is what counts. You have a way with horses. You have been born with it."'

His death, then, came as a shock. 'Jim Joel left some horses with Andy, who took over, including Maori Venture. A lovely ride. When he jumped off he would put his head nearly on the floor. Lad went straight over the top on him. He wasn't very big, never a good jumper. The National fences made him. Before Maori Venture, Bob had a young hurdler for Mr Joel. He had some ability. Bob wanted to make sure that Mr Joel, who was quite an old man by this stage, also saw him over fences, and he pushed on with him. He didn't think Mr Joel had long to live. In the end, Mr Joel outlived Bob.'

Moonax drew on all the talents Turnell had seen in Wallsgrove. 'People always had the wrong idea about Moonax,' she says. 'In his first race at Doncaster, his jockey, Richard Quinn, got knocked off him. Looking back, it seems bad – you know what people think about Moons, as I called him – but it wasn't his fault. In fact, we thought that the stewards would give us the race. Looking after him was fine. I took him on in the first place as the lad who looked after Moons as a two-year-old left and he was a spare for a while. That was partly because he already had all these quirks. I ended up taking him on top of my three at the time. I didn't think much of it, as the arrangement was temporary. In a short while I began to realise that there was actually another side to him. He wasn't as bad as everyone made out. After five months, I said to the guv'nor, "I've been looking after him all this time as a spare. Can I take him on as one of my three?" The guv'nor hadn't been that keen on a girl looking after him, but he must have thought, "Why not?"

'On the gallops, he wasn't so much a puller. Kevin Mooney, the ex-jumps jockey who was an assistant at Barry's, rode him quite a lot. What he did do was buck whenever he finished. That was the deal. At the races he wasn't too bad at all to me, just a bit snappy. He was fine with most other horses. In general, the issue was simply that he didn't really like horses or people around him or in his face. Certainly, you didn't take him on. He'd go at you for sure. In the beginning, I just ignored him. He must have thought, "She isn't like the others who always tell me off." Of course, if he pushed his luck I'd bring him into line. But he knew what for. We established boundaries and he knew to stay within them.'

Considering his problems, Wallsgrove rates Moonax as pretty brave. 'When he was a three-year-old he went to run in the Italian Derby. We had another horse running, called Rainbow Heights. Because of Moonax's reputation, it was decided to put him on the plane first, at the back, so no other horse would have to walk past him. It was actually Rainbow Heights who freaked. He just had a right wobble, and was throwing himself about. He pushed the middle partition between them on to Moons, who lashed out, as pretty much most horses would. The real problem was that he had caught his right hind leg between the partitions. The flying grooms were brilliant and jumped in to take Rainbow Heights off. But Moons was going down. I had to try and keep him up. We did get to Italy, but Moons' leg was swollen. I treated this by fermenting the injury with water for half an hour then walking him to stop the joint stiffening up. You might not imagine it, but he was a perfect patient for me, and on the journey home.

'After that, the leg was always a concern. It could also have been the reason why he seemed to try and duck out at Longchamp when he ran in the Prix du Cadran of 1996. All Frankie Dettori's fault. Ask him – he'll admit it. He did on the day. Before the race, we explained, "Don't hit Moonax on the right-hand side. That's the side where he has had all the trouble with his leg. Left side only, if you must." Of course, in the race he has his stick in his left hand. That was great. Then they came into the straight and he switched to the right. Gave Moons a smack. He took off sideways and headed for the gate that he remembered – he knew his way round Longchamp – took you back to the stables. Frankie said afterwards, "As soon as I hit him I thought about what you had said. I pulled my stick through and he flew after that. I threw away a Group One race. My fault – you told me not to do it. I completely forgot."'

No such problems in the St Leger in 1994. Moonax's leg and back – trouble there, too, pretty much throughout the colt's career – were both spot on. 'Winning a Classic didn't sink in to start off with,' says Wallsgrove. 'He was the outsider. Michael Hills had the chance to ride him but partnered Broadway Flyer for his brother, John. He'd beaten him in the Chester Vase, and that was the form choice. At Doncaster, Pat Eddery just had him lobbing along at the back. In the end he made up the ground by sneaking up the inner. During the race I was just talking to the other grooms. I was watching, but we were out the back door. I wasn't expecting anything spectacular. Then I saw him creeping up. Someone said, "He won't catch them." At that point they passed the furlong post. He stretched out his leg as if to say, "I'm going after this." I knew he wouldn't stop.

'Blues Traveller finished third in the 1993 Derby for me.

Placed in a Classic! Moonax's St Leger, the following year, was different, and not just because he won. Blues Traveller was in front for a while as he followed Tenby, who was favourite for the Derby, but then died and went backwards. They say, follow a fancied horse at Epsom, and Darryll Holland did the right thing. But at the front Blues Traveller lost his concentration and other horses were able to get back at him. With Moons, he was after those in front. He was catching up. He just chased them down. A lot more exciting, I can promise you. Not just for me. My sister missed the bingo for Moonax and had a pound each way.'

You'd forgive pretty much anything in return for a Classic. 'The only time Moons actually hurt someone in the yard,' Wallsgrove recalls, 'was when a lad went in to put on a bandage. Moons was in no mood for this and had a snap. The lad just said, "Leave it out." But Moons got hold of him and got him on the floor. Someone came along with a broom handle soon enough to scare him into letting the lad go. To be fair, the lad said, "My fault. Moonax told me to leave him alone." As for other horses, he did try and bite one in Paris. Moons ran against Always Earnest as a four-year-old in the Prix du Cadran – that race again! – of 1995. Always Earnest bumped him. That set Moons off. Pat Eddery, who usually rode him, thought we were the victims of that and he expected us to take the race in the stewards' room. We didn't. The guv'nor was pretty disappointed. He sided with Moons. "Think about it," he said. "What would you expect Eric Cantona to do if he was bumped?"'

*

A thorough grounding in horsemanship from the Turnells had prepared Wallsgrove for Moonax. Early Spring was a thrilling companion. Hurdlers such as Beacon Light and Birds Nest showed how horses could be restored to their best. 'Bob Turnell was so good at straightening them out after the Flat,' Wallsgrove says. 'He'd take sour horses and bring them round. The yard was in a village down from Peter Makin's place so he had the space in the countryside. Bob would take one up to watch the strings gallop on the Downs. Or he would take them off for a wander. They enjoyed it. On the way home, they would always stop for a pick at the grass.

'Beacon Light was an odd shape when he came to us off the Flat – no oil painting. Under Bob, he filled out. In schooling he would skim his hurdles; you'd never think that he could win over fences. He was also light-framed. Birds Nest had a lot of ability. On talent you would have to think that he'd win a Champion Hurdle. He was certainly a comedian. Steve Knight, the jockey, tried to jump up on him one day. He put one hand on his neck and the other behind the saddle and began to bounce up and down to jump on. While he was doing this, Birds Nest jumped when Steve jumped. He was just messing around. Even the guv'nor thought this was hilarious.'

Early Spring arrived as a fresh horse. 'He wasn't off the Flat. Spring – in the yard we shortened the name – arrived the season before me. He'd been broken through the winter of 1973 and I arrived in May 1974 just when he came back in. He was just a baby. No one wanted him anyway at first – too flashy: four white socks and a face. The head lad at the time, Taffy, said to me that he needed confidence, someone who could get on with him. He thought teaming up with Early Spring would do me good, as well as the horse. Spring was always a gentleman to me. I rode him every day in all his work. We grew up and learnt together.'

Everyone at Turnell's watched the partnership thrive. 'The guv'nor once asked me, "Can you hold him?" The answer was no. We just trusted each other. The familiarity we had meant he didn't run away with me. Quite a puller on the gallops. He'd put his head down. The key was knowing that you had to leave him alone. Andy Turnell would ask me, "How do I ride Early Spring?" He'd carry his head very low to the ground and didn't like it if you touched his mouth. Every now and then he would lift his head to see where he was going. If you touched his mouth with the bit then he would just take off. Andy rode very short – riding like that felt as if you were standing on top of the saddle – and if he went back in his seat, that could be a problem.

'When we schooled him he stood off his fences so far that it made it hard work for others who were also supposed to be learning. Instead, some of them picked up a style that was beyond their capabilities. He was so good over fences – a natural. Everything was so easy. That was what made him so devastating as a front runner. On the gallops he covered ground without seeming to do anything. He'd feel almost asleep under you. Everything was so smooth and felt effortless. It was like he wasn't taking anything out of himself.

'I'd take him home each summer, to his owner John Rogerson's place. The first year I took him back, the stud groom there said he couldn't believe how Spring had changed. "In the past, if you sneezed, he'd be off," he said. Now, after a season racing, his kids could play with him. It was all simply confidence.

'Spring always did test the fences every now and then. Most of his races he'd like to see how hard the fences were. He'd make a mistake and then sit tight for a bit. He never did like Cheltenham. He was favourite for the Champion Chase in 1978 but never threatened to win. He preferred places like Ascot. What he loved most was probably his food. He was running once at Lingfield and didn't eat up. I warned the guv'nor, who said, "See if he perks up when you arrive at the racecourse." He did a bit. In the end he won by five lengths. Afterwards, Mr Rogerson asked me, "How far would he have won by if he had been a hundred per cent?"'

*

After Bob Turnell's, Michael Dickinson at Manton was a contrast in style for Wallsgrove. 'They were still rebuilding at Manton when I arrived: four rows of ten boxes and two barns with room for twenty in total. In July 1985, when I started, we'd go to Robert Sangster's Swettenham Stud and collect the yearlings while they were finishing off what would eventually be their lodgings.

'It was starting from scratch. Michael Dickinson's ideas were totally different to anything that I had been used to. He had a lot of advisers. He was trying to set things up in an American style. He'd ask his work riders to gallop a certain number of seconds for every furlong. There were heart monitors; stride patterns were analysed and videoed. It was very scientific compared to Bob Turnell's. There were a couple of vets and every Thursday we'd have a trot up to see if there were problems. The most instinctive trick was turning the horses out for an hour in the paddock every day, including the colts. They had what we called a playpen. The fillies went out together. With Michael they'd all go out with New Zealand rugs. He used to say, "If they roll and get muddy then they are happy horses."

'Barry Hills' approach was more traditional. I looked after a filly called Snowkist. Michael Dickinson's verdict, based on her stride pattern, was that she was too small to win a race. Under Barry she won twice in 1987, first at Catterick then at Brighton. When punters saw her in the parade ring for the first time at Catterick I remember her odds walked, but she tracked like a greyhound. When she won again at Brighton, Cash Asmussen rode her. She carried a huge weight for a 14.3 hands filly. Cash came in afterwards and said that he had won by too far. He doubted she'd get up the hill with the weight and wanted to be sure there was enough in hand. "She's got a heart as big as a bucket," he said.'

Hills could be a tough taskmaster, though. 'Grumpy?

Mr Combustible? Oh yes! A bit of both, I think. You knew when he was on the warpath, and what he was looking out for. If he was in a mood you would make sure that the straps on the head collar were tucked in, and any cobwebs were cleared away. That they all had enough hay. The word went round: the boss is in a right mood. My yard was the furthest away from the main stable at South Bank so I had most time to find out how things were in the morning. Sometimes when he was shouting I would feel that the only name he knew was mine. A bugbear at South Bank was that I was sometimes slow out. With my barn furthest away, I was often last to the indoor school. I wouldn't hear the bell, which rang to say we were pulling out. I'd wait to see another barn pull out, which would mean I'd be behind from the start.

'I never saw the guv'nor untidy, or anything remotely out of place. Like the yard – always immaculate. Not a weed in the garden either. Mind you, I wouldn't want to be his golf caddy. Some of the Rupert Bear trousers he used to wear! And the caps! Penny Hills was always the peacemaker. She is the one who holds everything together and keeps the peace, does the apologising. The guv'nor used to give her a few bollockings too, though. I don't know how she puts up with it. She just adores him. Thinks the world of him.'

Underneath it all, however, there is a big heart. And he loved Snowkist. 'The guv'nor loved anything that tried,' Wallsgrove says, 'and even though she was a tiny little filly she gave everything. He'd say, "If this one had another hand in height, she'd be Triptych." She fractured her pelvis, which was almost because she just gave everything. Barry wouldn't let her go to stud until she was fine. She healed and everything, but the vets said the best thing for her was to be turned out so she could be exercised but not galloped. Rather than send her away, the guv'nor put a gate at either end of the area where we would trot up for Michael Dickinson. He wanted to be sure that Snowkist was fine before she went off to stud. He would go down there and give her carrots. Filled the space with straw, too. He's a softie really. He just doesn't like to show it.'

*

Bold Russian had a foot in Manton under Barry Hills in 1989, then in South Bank, when the trainer relocated. Exactly the sort of horse to smooth such a move. 'It was fortunate to have a good horse like Bold Russian in the yard when we went back to South Bank,' Wallsgrove says. 'He settled in all right after moving from Manton. A bit different to all those open spaces he was used to. He had horses coming back on him at South Bank as he went out on to the gallops. He'd never had that at Manton. He'd never been on the roads either. We'd also walk round the village, which he had never done at Manton. Actually, the change of environment wasn't a bad way of keeping him sweet.

'We called him Russell. He was just a lovely little horse. The guv'nor always really liked him. One night he came in with some owners. "As a rule, I am not too keen on Persian

Bold horses," he said. "But I do like this one. There is always a story behind a good horse. No one wanted this one. Michael Stoute turned him down, so did Henry Cecil. They seemed to think that others from the family weren't so nice."

'It never mattered to me what anyone else thought of Bold Russian. There was no malice in him at all. Happy, too. A right happy horse. He travelled to Ireland and France a few times. The flying grooms loved him, he was so well behaved. You always knew when he worked well: he'd do a German goose-step down the road. He was saying, "Look at me, I've done well. Good job."

'I took on Bold Russian because I had just lost a horse. The lad who was down to take him as a yearling had left Manton. Someone needed to take up the slack, so I said I would groom him and we'd see in the morning. The following day I was asked what I thought. If I didn't like him then he'd leave the yard. He was lovely, a real gentleman. I didn't want him to go.

'He developed quite slowly, though. He was a bit immature. He did seem to be shaping up to be quite sharp and won first time out, but he got much stronger as he got older. As a two-year-old he had a lot of problems, especially with his shoulders, which were sore a lot of the time. The thing was he actually preferred fast ground, overall, which meant it was difficult for him. I had a herbal remedy which I would rub into his shoulders. There was never any trouble with him while I was doing this. He'd be like a child's pony. He'd never harm anything.

'In the end, he went to America. You try to keep track, but finding the results is hard. Penny Hills was very good at keeping you up to date. You miss them, especially ones like Russell. He watched my back and would look out for me. When we did move back to Lambourn, Snowy, who was the head lad there, said to me, "You'll never sneak in late for work while he is in the yard. That horse is watching you everywhere. When you walk in every morning, he always shouts out hello."'

*

Blues Traveller gave Wallsgrove a taste of the big time at Epsom in 1993, a year ahead of Moonax. 'Blues took me to the Derby. He was second in the Dee Stakes, so I couldn't understand why he was 150–1 on the day. A few in the yard couldn't see why he was running. I said to them that there would be more finishing behind him than in front. And I was right.

'Before the race, he was improving. Every day he was getting better and better. Anyone could see that, especially me. You take a pride in your horse, and I was proud that Blues Traveller was good enough to run in the Derby. You get that lump in your throat when you do well. He could have been even better if he hadn't been so laid back and relaxed. At South Bank on the gallops there is a stretch that the guv'nor adapts to prepare horses for Epsom. They come down the side of the all-weather and then turn and go back up a little, in the shape of a horseshoe. They have to come down and round the bank so they learn a little bit about changing their legs and turning. Blues Traveller was being ridden by Darryll Holland. There were four of them. They all came down the all-weather and we were looking to see how they'd handle the turn. Then there were only three horses. Blues – another name we shortened around the yard – had just gone straight on down the gallop, as he usually would, and was on his way home. He was lobbing along behind the first three, nice and relaxed. He went to Epsom the day before for a spin round the real thing. Mr Hills also takes them to Chester ahead of the meeting. He likes them to get used to the tight track. It works, and it worked for Blues Traveller in the Derby too.

'After the Derby, Gary Tanaka bought him so he could run in the Del Mar Derby. I took Blues to California. When he was sold, Mr Hills asked me to. Well of course I'd accompany him. We had ten days on the road. There was quarantine in LA for two days. I was allowed to walk him up and down a corridor just to stretch his legs after 24 hours of travelling. When he got off the plane he was really wobbly. But he did well in America because he came back to a mile and a mile and one furlong. They fell in love with Blues Traveller. He had a brilliant temperament. Before the Del Mar Derby I rode him out on the track with a pony. He was sensible enough to stick to that pony like glue. American tracks in the morning are just organised chaos – a spaghetti junction of horses. They are everywhere. You feed on to the training track as best you can and the faster you go the nearer to the inside you should be. Luckily, I was told all this.'

Some time later, groom and colt were reunited in New Zealand. 'I went on holiday and visited the National Stud there in Cambridge,' Wallsgrove explains. 'I knew Blues had gone to New Zealand after a spell at stud in America and asked whether they had heard of him. In fact he was just down the road. He looked so well and laid back. I couldn't believe I was able to see him. He was leggy in training, but he had filled out. I talked with his groom about Blues' first crop, which hadn't run yet. In passing, I mentioned that at two he had fallen out of the stalls and been left ten lengths before rallying to finish third. While I was there he had his first two-year-olds runner in one of the trial races they have. The exact same thing happened: left at the start and finished fourth.'

*

Rainbow High was a cakewalk compared to Moonax. He stayed fresh, and any problems were swiftly solved. 'I took over Rainbow High as a four-year-old in 1999,' Wallsgrove says. 'At South Bank we had a new barn built, and I was head lad there. A girl looked after him at two, then another lad took over. Back problems were holding Rainbow up and I hadn't sat on him much up to the winter between three and four. Kevin Mooney said to me, "He needs help. He's pulling too much and is not right. He needs to go very steady and learn to relax. I want to see what you can do with him. Drop him out at the back of the string and lob along." So that's what I did.

'We solved one problem quite quickly, which was that he had been jumping off at the start. That was actually how he did his back in. He was now trying to run away from the pain. We let him hack for a winter, just a couple of months. I almost cried off him at that point. I could feel him strong underneath me. I thought, "He is going to go off on one soon. His problems will be back." Then the guv'nor asked me to work him on the grass, a proper gallop. I thought, "This is it – he'll run away with me." On the grass he would know it was work so he'd be wound up. Actually, everything just fell into place. He wasn't hurting, so he relaxed. Whether it was him or me I don't know. We suddenly had an idea of what we were supposed to be doing. There is no better feeling than having a problem horse come right. That feeling – we've done it! – is the best. From that point on we were fine. When he wasn't great or was a bit stiff, he'd start off slow, warm up a bit, then be ready to go. He knew himself what he wanted to do.'

Inevitably, Barry Hills looked at Chester. 'Rainbow loved Chester, that's for sure,' Wallsgrove continues. 'He just loved the turns there – anywhere really. The all-weather gallop up the Faringdon Road through our wood had a chicane in the middle, an S-bend. He loved it. When he was really right, you could feel him through there, changing legs. You really had to take a hold when he was that well. As for Ascot and the Gold Cup he never won, I think he just hated the place. I used to dread him running there. It was such a big, open track; Chester is tight, like our woods. Maybe it was fear of open spaces! He ended up with two Chester Cups. Credit to Mr Hills for keeping him fresh. He'd have long canters and pick up momentum and rhythm. That kept him sweet. He'd love his rolls in the sand pit, too, every day after he had exercised. At the back of the stables in the sand, that was where he was happy. As soon as his feet hit the sand he would go down.

'Barry Hills has always loved Chester. I don't know why he does. It was always a matter of what he would send. Sometimes you would think they had no chance, and they'd win. I don't know why they run well at Chester, but he obviously does.'

*

Leaving Barry Hills meant saying goodbye to Maids Causeway. Luckily, in her new role at Newmarket, Wallsgrove can expect to see familiar faces, including the filly. Her departure to fill the post of racecourse stables manager at headquarters also meant leaving the bosom of an extended family. 'I can't pick the Hills twins, Richard and Michael,' Wallsgrove says. 'Michael is the one who speaks to me the most, as I know him better, so if one of them is talking to me I know it's usually Michael. I know the next generation well – Charles, assistant to Barry, and George. I saw them grow up from nothing. And I have known Darryll Holland since he started as an apprentice. He was part of my team. I gave him a right slap once for being cheeky. He was just showing off. I walloped him. He was better after that and did come up to me once to say, "I have to thank you for those days."

'Darryll was a natural, from the start. Like a good horse, it is just a case of bringing it out. Of all the other apprentices we had, he was the one you knew would make it. The others would ride winners, for sure, but he was always going to be special. You could see. It's the same with a good horse, the feel that they give you. When Darryll was young, he was cheeky and he'd be showing off in front of his mates. But he also wanted to learn. Not just about the riding, but, why did you do this, why did you do that, how about this, how about that? Like Peter Chapple-Hyam at Manton. To Darryll, there was a deep side. He questioned things, just like Peter. They both want to know – not just yes and no, but why? That was the difference between Darryll and the others. Some apprentices think they are good and that they don't need to learn, that they have had it all given to them.

'I'd expect to see a bit of Peter, who now trains in Newmarket. Back at Manton, he was a bit like Darryll, as well as being a big teddy bear. As an assistant trainer he knew what he was doing and where he was going. He took everything in and was not frightened to ask questions. He's not stupid at all. He has that jolly, happy-go-lucky outlook. But underneath he is a deep thinker. A smashing bloke who would do anything for you.'

Wallsgrove did see Maids Causeway, for she came to

Newmarket in 2005 for the 1,000 Guineas. 'She was a difficult old filly,' Wallsgrove recalls. 'Kevin Mooney wanted me on her because she was quite free and he didn't want her being overgalloped by one of the lads. She was always jumping about, and she kicked and bucked too. Was never still. It took her a while to get the hang of things after her first run. The guv'nor saw her larking around one day and said, "I'll give her something to think about. I'll run her." It was the beginning of June and she wasn't really ready – got beaten a head by another one of ours at Newbury. The guv'nor realised after she ran that she must be a nice filly as she ran so well without being that experienced. Before I'd told him, "She's nice." "I'll give her nice," he said. In time, the guv'nor saw her in a different light. Closed his eyes to the naughty bits.

'In the 1,000 Guineas, she didn't see Virginia Waters, who came from off the pace to win. She made ground back as soon as she saw her ahead. When you rode her you couldn't fight her. She would take you on every inch of the way. And you wouldn't want to take that away from her, or dampen the competitor in her.'

Wallsgrove's thoughts turned back to Moonax, another who boasted a big heart. 'For mucking out, I'd come in with the straw to spread it around. He would help by grabbing the stuff in his mouth and shaking it out for me. Sometimes he would be really low, just flat. He'd stick his head under your arm and just wanted a cuddle. Then he'd be fine and shake himself down, as if to say, "I'm not a softie or anything like that, you know. You can leave me alone again."

'When I was in his box and someone came to the door to have a chat, he'd brush up against me while we were talking. He'd push over towards you. People would think that he was going to kick. I always said he wasn't, and he never did. He just liked to feel you. It was the same when you filled up the water mangers in the corner of the boxes. If everyone was filling up this could take ages. He'd just move over towards you, backside first. I knew he wouldn't kick. He'd just lean over. I'd slip my leg round his so he knew I was there. He liked the contact.

'He only bit me once, in Ireland, after he ran in the St Leger there. It was supposed to rain but there wasn't a drop. Moons heard his feet rattle in the race and at the finish was lame. In a foul mood too. We had to yank his saddle off him. The vet asked to have a look. He'd have been lucky to make it inside the box, let alone examine Moons. I said, "No one should go near him." For a moment I wasn't looking, and he caught my arm. Wouldn't let go. It ended up swollen from the shoulder to the wrist. I spent four hours in casualty.

'Sometimes he would stick his tongue out at you. And he loved it when you rubbed his teeth and gums. People thought I was mad to put my hand anywhere near his mouth. If you knew why he liked having his gums rubbed, you'd see that there was nothing wrong with it at all. He just liked the calming effect. It helped him relax. When he was grumpy, I'd do what had to be done and leave him alone.

You couldn't push him out of a mood. You just had to wait until it passed.

'There were other silly habits. We once tried to put some special tack on him. Every time we reached down to slip on his girth, Moons would pull away the special tack. So we'd leave the girth and get back a hold of the special tack. Then when we picked up the girth again Moons grabbed the special tack again. This went on for ten minutes. In the end, Moons just stood there looking at us. He was saying, "I've got you."

'I quit Barry Hills because you get to a stage where you cannot keep riding the awkward horses. You have to find something else to do. I wouldn't have been able to sit by when a Moonax came along, and just ride the easy ones. If there was one who needed riding or looking after, I'd want to do it. So I had to turn my back on it. I didn't want to get to the stage where I was frightened. Some in yards are terrified. I never wanted to be crying off. Not when I'd experienced the likes of Moonax and how rewarding it can be when a horse like him comes right. Moons and me, we grew together. I ignored him and all his nonsense at first, and he realised he could trust me. Then he took some interest in what I was doing, so I would pay attention to him. It became a partnership.'

CHAPTER THREE

LARRY POLAND

Hallo Dandy and a lifetime at Greystoke

Larry Poland has racing in his genes. The two preceding generations of his clan had loved racing, so naturally enough he gave the game a go. Now near the end of his career, Poland has two Grand National winners against his name in Hallo Dandy and Lucius. His ancestors would be just as proud that Poland grew over 30 years into a key figure at the Greystoke stables of the late Gordon Richards.

So he ended up at one of the north's great seats of jumping power, but as a teenager, south seemed the right direction for this proud Scot. That was the way he headed, with Ryan Price's yard in mind. He'd followed the trainer's horses from afar, so one day he rang him up, as you do. Poland was a bit brash back in the 1960s, he admits. A bit of a chancer, too: he said he could ride. In the end, the game did come naturally. On the gallops with Price in the company of Josh Gifford, stylish stable jockey of the day, and Paul Kelleway, Gifford's understudy, Poland was soon on his way. By the time he was established as a permanent fixture at Greystoke he'd evolved from the Long John Silver jockey-style of his early days, fit only for the hunting field, into the safest pair of hands.

Before 'Dandy', Greystoke and Gordon Richards, there were a few stopovers. A difference of opinion with Captain Price over afternoons spent picking stones off the gallops meant a journey home for a couple of months. Then Poland hit the road, thumbed a lift, and recrossed the border to Scotch Corner. After a night sleeping in an old hay barn, he scrubbed up well enough to score a job in Middleham with Sam Hall, staying on with Sally when Sam moved yards. Spells with Ken Oliver and Harry Bell, on the other side of Hadrian's Wall again, followed.

Poland's arrival at his final destination of Greystoke came after three years out of the game. Poland left Harry Bell to learn JCB driving in Hawick. After that he joined his brother in Epsom and worked as a polisher of Ronson lighters at the company's Leatherhead factory. The money was £100 a week, compared with his starting salary with Richards of around a tenth of that. Ultimately the economics were less of a consideration than quality of life. Poland simply missed the racing too much.

Greystoke was a place to settle. Poland had always studied the Form Book, and ahead of him were the entries Lord Greystoke, Unguided Missile, Clever Folly and Addington Boy – winners, respectively, of the Cathcart (1981), the National Hunt Chase (1998), the AF Budge Gold

Cup (1989) and the Tripleprint Gold Cup (1996). In 1990, Four Trix added a Scottish National to Richards' Aintree versions, and Noddy's Ryde was prolific as a novice chaser before being taken by injury. One Man raised the bar further with a Queen Mother Champion Chase in 1998 and before that the King George twice, in the process generating plenty of debate about his precise merits. Rinus could have been a National winner, Poland suggests; he finished third in 1990 and was then cruelly halted in his prime. Maybe, too, Rinus would have won a Gold Cup, given the chance.

Behind the success, the work was hard. In the early days, the hours were seven a.m. till one p.m. with breakfast after nine for half an hour. You'd then be back for two hours of evening stables, finishing before six p.m. most days, all being well. Luckily, Poland was never alone in setting the standard. Sharing the morning workload over the years have been jockeys such as Jonjo O'Neill, Ron Barry, David Goulding, Neale Doughty and Phil Tuck – the very best of horsemen, notes Poland. A brace of National winners is, at the very least, some reward for enduring tough times, for there have also been sad days. Sea Pigeon's departure from Greystoke to Peter Easterby's yard for one, well before the gelding's greatest moments. There was the shock, too, in learning, long into what should have been Hallo Dandy's well-earned retirement, that the hero of Aintree in 1984 had been left in a field, neglected by uncaring custodians. Well done to the Thoroughbred Rehabilitation Centre for the rescue of Dandy, says one of his oldest friends.

This journey in racing could have stalled with a first fall. 'When I called Captain Price on the telephone,' Poland recalls, 'he asked me what I knew. Obviously I said I could ride, which was a lie. First morning, I was handed this tack. I asked a lad, "Help me with this – it's a bit different to what I'm used to." That bit was fine. But when they gave me a leg up, I ended up over the top on the other side.' Forty years on, the memory is starting to fade just a touch, Poland concedes. 'In my younger days I could tell you the breeding and what they had done. At Gordon's, and with Nicky, his son, who took over when the boss died in 1998, a lot came to us where we'd looked after their mothers.' Poland hopes to see a few more generations yet. 'I'll carry on at least until next week, when I win the lottery. I can get fed up when I think my time's not my own. Just the five days a week would be nice. We also get only four weeks off, and I am on the same money as someone who comes in at the age of 21. But, to be truthful, I still enjoy it. I am riding today better than I did twenty years ago. I've ridden all the rough ones. The trick is where you sit in the saddle, and where your hands are – drop them down and give a bit of rein. Also, your manner is important. You shouldn't gather them up; they'll only feel bullied. It's all about experience. You pick that up over time.'

*

Poland may reckon that he rides better now than two decades ago, but his hands were already good enough for

Hallo Dandy before the 1984 Grand National. 'Dandy could be a bit boisterous before a gallop,' Poland says. 'He would get het up waiting to go. That was always his way. I've seen him at parades for the National since he was retired. It's obvious just from those that he was a handful – really hard to control. He'd become a bit edgy when he knew there was something coming up, especially when he was well. He wanted to get on with things. Gordon would say, "You lead us, Larry – just a canter." I'd go off and we'd make nice progress, then I'd look behind me and we'd be miles ahead of anything else. "We can't catch you, Larry," the boss would complain. Too quick for the rest of them, I'd say. He was a beautiful mover – a big, long-striding horse who really covered the ground.' He needed watching though. 'One day, I went into his box for something and Dandy shot straight out the door. He usually just stood there, calm as anything, while I went about things. For some reason on this day he was gone, out of the stables. I just managed to grab on to his tail. We went out of the yard over a wall and across from where the castle is, with me still hanging on. He was galloping off down the castle drive and I was shouting "Whoa there!" at the same time taking huge strides to keep with him as he was a big horse. He eventually pulled up round the corner. Lucky, as the National was soon enough. The old heart was going. Who knows where he would have finished up?'

The Hall of Fame at Aintree was Hallo Dandy's destiny. 'He came from Ginger McCain's,' Poland continues. 'He had won over fences and was reckoned to have set a new track record at Haydock as a novice chaser, so we were plenty glad to have him. A guy called Ross looked after him. Dandy finished fourth in 1983 in the National, then Ross left, so I got landed with him while he recovered from the race. The boss said, "Take care of him for now." He actually got a bit colicky after his first run in the National as the race had been a tough one. At first I walked him for two, sometimes three miles on the road to help him get over this. When he was ready to come back into training proper, Pat, the head man, asked me to look after him. "No thanks," I said. "Don't be daft," Pat told me. "He's going for the National again." So I started to ride him out. Then he bolted up at Ayr.

'We really fancied him in 1984. We travelled to Aintree on the day. The journey was only two hours, but we left at half seven to beat the traffic. I knew he would win. A couple of days before they raced Gordon would always school them. It was the same for Dandy ahead of the National. A good pop a couple of weeks ahead of the race, then again the day before, just once over the fences to get his eye in. He was a natural. The leap he took over Becher's Brook in the National? Well! And over the Canal Turn? He was like a deer. We didn't go back to the yard afterwards. Went to the village instead and let Dandy out of the box so everyone could see him. I remember we had two other winners on the day, and the local pub was packed – everyone from the yard, which was thanks to Gordon for covering the expense – except for the town's bookmaker, Archie, a real rascal. The race almost broke him.

I'd told him, "You want to be on the right side of this one." He was giving out 25–1 when he was a good bit less than that. He ended up selling his car to cover everything. Richard Shaw, Dandy's owner, was very careful with his money. Just £2,000 between everyone, jockey and trainer included. I only got a little bit – certainly nothing to shout about. Not enough, for sure, to buy Archie's car off him.'

Dandy had proved himself to be a true Aintree specialist. 'You'd start to plan for the next one straight away,' Poland says. 'He was a natural, like Red Rum. He liked the course and always jumped really well. You couldn't ask for better. Even in his fourth National he could have won if he hadn't been nearly brought down. He was just making his ground when he was almost taken out. At the time, Neale Doughty just did very well to stay on. The only time Dandy fell in the National was the year after he won the race. For that, he was the best we had ever had him. For the fall, I blamed the jockey. He'd been told to stay in the middle to outer. He jumped off last. When he jumped the first, he passed seven in the air he was going so fast. Graham Bradley, that was. He ripped some ligaments in his shoulder and was off for a few months. I said a few things about him that day. I just couldn't forgive him. Dandy looked twice the horse he had been the year before. He didn't sweat up and was really bolshie before the start, ready to race. Looked a million dollars. Dick Pitman wandered over and said how well he looked. How I didn't win the best-turned-out prize I'll never know.

'When he won his first National he had been suffering from a high protein count. In the weeks before the race he'd started to look very dull in his coat, which the vet said was a result of his diet. He looked too lean so his feed had to be changed. They had to cut back what he was eating two weeks before the race and give him a bit more work. You don't want to overfeed them. That's when they start to burst blood vessels. He had a few problems in his time. In between his second and third National he developed a leg – tendon trouble – after spending some time on the beach. Whether he hit something and strained it or stumbled I just don't know. But he got over that.'

Mercifully, Dandy is now enjoying a happy retirement. 'He's at the Thoroughbred Rehabilitation Centre. I'm so glad he has a good home. What happened to Dandy after he retired shouldn't be allowed. He was just roughed out in a field with no hay – nothing over the winter. I saw him at Carlisle a while back. Much the same as I remember him. He looked well, and that's important. Back opening shops and things. They don't remember you, horses. You'd like to think that they do, but they don't, whatever anybody says. But I still know the old Dandy.'

Poland considers Lucius a match for Hallo Dandy. 'Lucius was always very game, very honest, would give of his best every time. With him, I just laugh at the memory. I can't help but think of Wacky Races. He just reminded me of the cartoon character Muttley. Lucius would always be sniggering away.' Like Dandy, Lucius also needed watching. 'He was like Houdini. He could get out of anywhere. When I got married we lived in a separate yard about four miles away from the main stables. I looked after about half a dozen and would ride them out and then do the road work with them before they returned to training. Just six to eight weeks to give them a break. I'd ride about four of them out every morning. The lads would bring me hay and stuff. I was pretty much left to my own devices. Lucius had been running in novice handicap hurdles when I took him in. He was about to go novice chasing. He was a real character. He'd open his own stable door. They opened into the boxes, big heavy things, and there was a bolt that went nine inches into the wall. He'd look to see if anyone was coming. My window was right next to his door. I'd watch him as he took a peek. Then, if he thought he was in the clear, he'd use his foot to knock the bolt out and pull the door back with his teeth. A proper old stable door, and he'd pull the damn thing open!

'Most days I caught him, but one night my wife and I went to a party. It was pitch black when we returned and I presumed he was there. But the bugger had gone. In the morning I rang Gordon – not a phone call I enjoyed. "Lucius has disappeared," I said. "What exactly do you mean?" Gordon asked. I did my best to explain. He never galloped off, he'd just walk, and this time he'd just strolled up to the next village and gone into someone's garden. We found out which one and the owner, a lady, said she had chased him out. He'd moved on to a field and was standing there with a donkey, picking at the grass. He'd jumped over a wall to get in.

'Another time he went missing before evening stables, and everyone was looking for him. Two old ladies were coming down the road so we asked them if they had seen a loose horse. "Oh yes," they said, "but we thought he knew where he was going as he had a coat on." Coming up the castle drive to work, you would see him on the front lawn, just standing there picking at the grass. Then you'd realise he was on his own. He'd got out again.

'He took a fair old hand. Doddsy, the lad who looked after him, would sit behind me on the way to the gallops as otherwise he'd whip round and be off. To turn on to the gallops you'd take a sharp left, so I'd block the way so that he couldn't just spring away. He practically went straight through me a good few times.'

Like Dandy, Lucius fulfilled his potential, in 1978. 'I dreamt before the National that Lucius won it,' Poland reveals, 'except there was no jockey on him. This was before David Goulding got injured and Bob Davies took over. I didn't say anything. Everyone would have thought I was daft.' Rinus, whom Poland rates ahead of both Lucius and Hallo Dandy, was less fortunate. 'Rinus, he was a different class,' he says. 'He had a wind problem, but he still won a hatful of novice chases, and the Greenall Whitley Gold Cup. The trouble was a soft palate. Remember when he ran in the National in 1990? Four from home, he was cantering but started to gargle. He could easily have won that day, but he was really a Gold Cup horse: a very good jumper, very quick, very precise.

'After Rinus finished third in the National in 1990, we were getting him ready for the race again. He was due a run before Aintree, over hurdles to get fit. He led some of the best three-mile hurdlers a merry dance at Haydock. Then he got tired and started to gargle again. We said to the owners, "He really needs to have his wind done" – a tie-back. The procedure worked really well. Then he was taken off to Kelso for a run ahead of the National, but it was too firm. So we went to Bangor, where the ground was perfect. But he struck through his tendon and had to be put down. Very sad for everyone at the yard. Without the wind problem he'd have won at Cheltenham, for sure. At home he was always a real gentleman, a lovely horse and a real character. If you were dressing him over, he'd look round at you as if to say, "What have you got for me? Pay attention. Have you got a polo?" A really handsome horse. On the gallops, you knew that you were partnering class. They give you this feel, like driving a Rolls-Royce instead of an old Ford. It was evident right from the start when he came to us at about five. Like Hallo Dandy, another one from Ginger McCain. Good enough to win a National too.'

*

Gordon Richards and Ryan Price – tough taskmasters to all who passed through their hands. 'Gordon was very tough and strict,' Poland recalls. 'Only after a good few years would he begin to ask you about the ones you looked after. What's the matter with this one? Maybe he isn't fit or it's the bad back? He tried lots of different things to get the best out of horses, and was a very good judge. Still, he always liked to keep you under the thumb. His son, Nicky, is different – a different way with the horses. With Gordon we used the big hill a lot, and there was plenty of speed work. With Nicky it's three times up the mile gallop, nice and steady, while the boss – I still call Gordon that – was more two-furlong dashes. He'd give them a real blow with quick runs up the hill. Nicky is finding his own way. He is quiet. Not like his father. A real sergeant-major type.

'Ryan Price was also tough, ex-army, but fair with it. If you looked after a winner he'd say to the owner, "Give the lad a drink." He made sure you were looked after. Sure he was a shouter and a bawler, but not at me. I was quiet. I had a very broad accent but he could follow me. One day I was picking stones out of my horse's feet when he came into the box. He kicked me right up the backside. I asked him, "What was that for?" "I want you stood to attention by the horse when I come in," he said.

'Gordon was great at keeping his horses fresh. He'd use so many different gallops that they never got fed up. At Greystoke there is a roundabout from which you can do two canters. Just down from the roundabout there is a valley, or you can round the hill two or three different ways to reach the moor. That's plenty of variety.

'We'd always end up riding the rough ones. Gordon

would say, "You come with us, Larry." "Are you sure, boss?" I'd say. "Yes. You start out the back." Next minute you are flying past horses. I remember once when Pat Kavanagh was riding out with me and Gordon was on Pyjamas. Remember him? The old handicap chaser. Gordon said, "Come on you two, we need to go as fast as we can." Pat's horse was one of those who whipped around a lot so I waited with him at the start. Gordon was off ten lengths, shouting, "Come on, lads, come on!" We looked at each other, smiled, and went off after him, either side. In no time we flew past. At the top of the gallops Gordon couldn't speak he was so tired. He finally got his breath back. "You buggers! I said go as quick as you can, but not that quick."'

'At Ryan Price's, Paul Kelleway and Josh Gifford were the tearaways. Josh was in a couple of car crashes and could have been killed. He was good with the lads. Jockeys were in those days. He would give you a few quid if you had a winner. Josh was a real professional. I still think he is the best I have ever seen. Him, Terry Biddlecombe and the rest – all better than anything riding at the moment. They were proper horsemen. Remember that Josh was champion apprentice on the Flat. At Greystoke, Neale Doughty was the best horseman I ever saw over fences. Better even than Josh at presenting a horse to jump. Also a lunatic! Typical Welshman. He was always a bit bullish and loved to celebrate. He was always doing pranks. Up the gallops, he'd come one side, with maybe Ron Barry on the other side. They'd lift you out of the irons. With Ron it was very difficult to know what he was saying with his Irish accent. Very hard to follow. Jonjo O'Neill? He couldn't have been more different. You never heard him swear and he didn't drink either. Always very quiet, like Phil Tuck, who was more the gentlemanly type. Jonjo lived with Gordon before he got married. He never went gallivanting or anything like that. A lovely fellow.'

*

There have been few years at Greystoke without something to quicken the pulse. Plenty of people had an opinion about One Man, but not much attention was paid to folk beyond Greystoke. 'We didn't waste much time on what people would say about One Man,' Poland says. 'There weren't many in the game who didn't have a view. We always thought he was going to be a Gold Cup horse. To me, he used to break blood vessels, including at home. At the races, when he was beaten he simply stopped too quickly. People would see him run and say that he didn't stay, but to me he was always breaking and that was why he just stopped so suddenly. He'd be on the bridle coming to the second last, then stop straight there. At the racecourse we only saw it once, at Aintree, when he finished with his nostrils full of blood. At the yard, never. I'd always ask, "Has that horse got any blood in his bucket?" In those days we didn't scope them. Some would say, "The trouble with One Man is that when he runs he's not fit." Well, I could see why they might say that – he was a big, barrelly sort of horse. Remember that he was probably better fresh. Maybe if the boss had done things different he would not have won the races that he did – the King George, the Queen Mother Champion Chase. If you have a breaker and are hard on him, then you won't win anything at all. It all depends on how you train them.'

Whatever his limitations, One Man was a thrilling ride. 'He was always a beautiful jumper,' Poland continues. 'He'd get excited when he knew he was going out to be schooled or for a gallop. He'd be dragging you up the road with him. He could be quite a handful. He wasn't a broad horse, just big. He was built a bit like a sprinter on the Flat. He wasn't as tall as you might think from the way he jumped. He'd be lucky to be sixteen hands. He had short legs but was big-bodied, and strong. His jumping came from having great strength behind the saddle, and he was a natural. Just the odd mistake. I remember he nearly unseated Tony Dobbin at Haydock. Gordon gave Tony a right bollocking for that, but it wasn't Tony's fault at all.

'I rode him twice when he was young. The boss said, "You take him today." He was another who felt like a Rolls-Royce. You can tell right away. A different type to Rinus. Maybe Rinus just had a little bit more speed. But One Man always had a lot. He'd be quite boisterous, and keen. He took quite a hold up the gallops. Gordon – all twelve, thirteen stone of him – used to ride him like he did all the good ones. Once he knew they were good, he'd be on them. He didn't slow down One Man, mind.

'For the yard to have a good one was always a great

boost. We usually had the quality, going right back to Sea
Pigeon, The Spaniard and Titus Oates, who was in the yard
the day I joined. We all knew Sea Pigeon was good. He'd
managed to finish seventh in the Derby, after all. I think he
cost about £28,000, which was a lot of money in those days
when you were on £9 a week. I rode him just the once, the
first day he was with us. I went down on the roads with him.
It was only a walk, but it meant that I could always say I was
the first lad to sit on him.

'With Clever Folly, getting him off the mark was the
hard bit. At first we couldn't win a race with him. He was
being held up at the back of the field – nothing. He was due
to go to the sales in a week. The last time he was due to run
for us, the boss said to let him go at the tapes. He hacked up.
We kept him after that and he went on from there. I think he
broke the track record at Cheltenham. He was always very
keen. He used to run away with Gordon. "Right, lads, a nice
canter now," Gordon would say. Then he'd be off and you
wouldn't see him until after the gallops.

'Four Trix was a contrast. Very straightforward, quiet
and easy to handle. He had a lot of ability – enough to win
the National itself, I'd say. But he wasn't the best jumper. It
is what happens on the day, and his day was at Ayr. A
Scottish National instead.

'A lad called Tommy looked after Noddy's Ryde. He
actually came to the yard with the horse. He was a terrible
ride: he would run away with you. The boss said one day,
"I'll ride him." Tommy said, "You don't want to be doing

that, boss." The horse ran away with him. It was a real shame that he broke a leg at Exeter as he would have gone right to the top.

'Unguided Missile was just very naughty. A girl started out looking after him but after a few days she wanted out as he would charge at her. A fellow called Big Jack took over. He squared up to him. After that, he was fine. I think he fancied himself as the boss. He was just naughty, just a baby. When they are like that you look for what is wrong. In his case it was a murmur with his heart. They ran him at Kelso for the first time over fences and he was staggering all over the place afterwards. A shame that we lost him at Ascot when the heart packed in.

'Addington Boy's best moment was in 1996 at Cheltenham in the Tripleprint Gold Cup. I took him on at the end of his career. He had problems with his legs which made getting him fit tough. He also used to get very dehydrated. In the wagon, he would sweat and sweat. At the races he might be fine; then, as soon as you began to put on the tack, he'd start to sweat again. He'd need extra salts and he was a bit vulnerable to the virus.

'I looked after Lord Greystoke from the days when he was a baby. He was a big, fat thing and no one would take him, so I said I would. He had no badness in him at all and you could tell from riding him that there was something about him. As he grew older he became more and more confident. Going down the drive, he'd walk on his back legs, which was quite a sight. I taught him the basics – how to walk, how to gallop, how to use himself and his stride. He was pretty much Flat-bred; his name was changed for jumping. He was always honest. He went to Dickinson's at the age of eleven. By then a bit of arthritis had set in. You do get attached to them, and it is disappointing when they go. I'd say that it's like someone taking your kid away from you. Lord Greystoke was one of my favourites, I would have to say. Him, Rinus and Dandy.'

*

Horses remain the challenge for Larry Poland. McGregor the Third won back-to-back Sporting Index Chases at Cheltenham in November 1996 and January 1998. Then, in the same race the following season, he ducked out under Tony Dobbin. This was no surprise to Poland. The gelding did that all the time at home, he confesses.

Horses take some knowing, says Poland. 'We had one who would just bolt, flat out, without any warning. He'd be running for his life down a road. That's scary. You had to take him round the hills to the gallops as he couldn't go with the others. We were at Chepstow with him one day and the lad who had come with me asked to lead him up for the extra money. I knew what the horse was like so I said OK. They ended up stuck at the top of this grass bank. The lad shouted at me, "You bastard! You knew that would happen!" There were tears running down my face. "You shouldn't be so greedy," I said.'

Like Rinus, not all fulfil their potential. 'Edelweis du

Moulin was another who did his best to overcome leg problems,' Poland continues. 'He should have won the Arkle in 1998. The plan that day was hold him up, hold him up, hold him up. In fact he was a potential Gold Cup horse, a stayer, so when the rest quickened he couldn't go with them. If he had quickened earlier he would have had a chance.'

Some things in the game have changed, some have stayed the same. 'I don't know whether it's the flu injections,' Poland says, 'but these days you see horses getting sick, coughing, breaking blood vessels. In past days they fed horses corn and bran, and added eggs, Guinness. Maybe it is high-protein feed. For all their size, horses are very vulnerable. Good, bad, whatever, they can all have problems. It doesn't matter if they have a smooth action. Sometimes you think the good ones are the most trouble.' Horses, Poland reckons, are just like people. 'They can have their own way, and it is their way all right. You talk to them. You get fond of them, looking after them day after day, week after week. Some try and kick you and bite, and then you think, "Why are they like that?" No point in knocking them around. If I see that at the yard, I say, "Hey, there are other ways to work that out." Nothing more than a slap. It is probably because they have got something wrong with them. You have to be patient. Always try to find out why. Like in life.'

CHAPTER FOUR
DENNIS WRIGHT

*Shirley Heights and the best of times
with John Dunlop*

Dennis Wright has a plan: when the time comes, he'll retire to the Costa Blanca. Yet a little bit of home will always be in Arundel, at John Dunlop's stable. Wright began work there in 1963. In those days his guv'nor was the racing secretary, typing away with one finger.

Wright has been at Arundel for over 40 of his near half-century of years in the game. In that time he has also managed to clock up eleven marathons, and has proudly worn the Sussex County athletics vest. Even now, with retirement pending, he remains most interested in what tomorrow holds. 'Every year, when the yearlings are broken – 80 of them – that is exciting,' he enthuses. 'I've known their mothers, their grandmothers, most of the families. If they have a quirk, you'll remember the mother sharing it. Spring's the best time of the year. A full yard, which is important, and maybe a champion among them.' That thought is enough to guarantee that Wright, resident near the yard and Arundel Castle, is up the hill for 4.30 a.m. to give the string breakfast. Then he's back home for his own – tea, toast and sight of the news. After that he returns to the yard to straighten any rugs and tidy up boots and bandages. To finish the morning, he rides three lots before lunchtime. 'There's a start to the day in racing,' Wright accepts, 'but there's never a finish time.'

He has grown into the job since school days, when his nickname was 'Titch'. At Jack Collings' West Ilsley stables, where he was given his first job in racing, Wright became 'Tiger' after the star South African jockey of the day. The grand total of three shillings and sixpence a week was the pay, plus a bus fare to Newbury, and ten shillings a year to buy clothes. The wages were usually spent by Sunday night, either gambled or drunk. A lift to Newbury on the horsebox during the winter allowed him the chance to see a motion picture, as they called films back in those days.

When Wright looks back at the progress made at Arundel, there is plenty to admire, not least the evolution of a yard from 40 horses to one of the land's great seats of racing power. Ragstone, the Gold Cup winner at Royal Ascot in 1974, gave the stable a taste of the big time, then Shirley Heights provided a Classic feast with Epsom and Irish Derbies in 1978. Six years later Circus Plume won the Epsom Oaks. In the seasons since then there has been another Epsom Derby – Erhaab in 1994 – and the Irish version to match Shirley Heights' own success from Salsabil in 1990. She also recorded two other Classics: the Oaks again, and the 1,000 Guineas at Newmarket. This reflected the horsepower brought to the yard by the Maktoums.

At the racecourse, Pat Eddery and Willie Carson have steered a host of leading lights which Wright helped prep at home. Together, these jockeys in particular have played their part in securing Arundel's position today as one of Britain's premier stables. Both Eddery and Carson seem to have been part of Arundel almost for as long as Wright. Eddery's saddle fitted Silver Patriarch, successful in the 1997 St Leger, and Millenary, who by the end of 2004 had Doncaster and Yorkshire Cups to his name as well as the Princess of Wales's Stakes and, of course, a St Leger. Before Silver Patriarch and Millenary, Carson memorably held on to Habibti with her 'gears' to win the July Cup, Nunthorpe, Vernons Sprint and Prix de l'Abbaye in 1983. Carson took the less-travelled road twelve years later on Bahri at Ascot for a memorable Queen Elizabeth II Stakes success.

An incredulous Wright watched Bahri's QEII back at the yard as the jockey left the pack and boldly – that's with hindsight – took the outside rail. 'Horses like him can surprise you,' he concedes. 'As a two-year-old he was second three times. That normally means they won't turn out to be something special. He was a big, weak-looking horse. I think he was just trying to find his feet. He had the frame but he needed to mature. He showed us on the gallops that he had talent and he was a good worker, but he was unfurnished. He just needed time. Along the way, he was a really nice guy. In the box, out of the box, he was one of those horses you couldn't fault. After a while, for all the nice work he did, I began to wonder. You begin to think, "Where is the extra for the racecourse?" In his case, that came with maturity. He flourished over the winter and with each race he'd come on. You would see it physically, and in work. "One step at a time," Mr Dunlop says,' Wright adds with a laugh.

When Wright was travelling horses for Dunlop as the trainer pioneered the art of continental raiding, there could be five-hour waits dockside. Sometimes Wright would have a party of ten heading for Cagnes-sur-Mer and the spring season there. The sea was partly why Wright took such a shine to Arundel. But John Dunlop, who took over from Gordon Smyth in 1966, is the main reason he has stayed so long. Together, over the years, they have faced a range of questions posed by a range of equine personalities. In some cases, a tricky nature was self-evident from racecourse antics. Yet even today Carson would be bewildered to learn the truth about Chilibang, who was a saint at the track but the trickiest of customers for Wright back home. At least he delivered when it mattered. 'I've seen plenty who then don't perform at the races,' says Wright. 'Morning glories. They fly up the hill, then flop on the track. I'm used to that now. I just wait for the next good one.'

*

With every year that passed, Arundel grew into the stable it is today, and the very best came thicker and faster for

Dennis Wright. Ragstone's Ascot Gold Cup in 1974 was the first sign that Wright's place of work would rate among racing's great powerhouses of his generation. The yard's status as a top-ranking stable was further enhanced by Balmerino, second in the Arc in 1977, and other high-end performers such as North Stoke, one of Dunlop's pioneer winners in five countries including Belgium and Germany. Four years on from Ragstone, Shirley Heights' success in the Derby confirmed Arundel's arrival in the big time.

'We knew Ragstone had stamina,' Wright reflects, 'but you wouldn't have picked him out as a potential Gold Cup winner. When he won the Gold Cup we had about 40 horses, and his owner, the Duke of Norfolk – he lived in the castle – was the main man and patron. As he was the Queen's representative at Royal Ascot, he'd always wanted to win the Gold Cup, much more than the Derby. You talk about parties like the one we had after Shirley Heights won the Derby. This was a big party, in the castle, for everyone, including the whole estate's workforce. A very nice horse, though he was a little bit keen. That's strange for a stayer, but he settled in the end.

'Any Ascot winner is top notch for the yard. For the week, we all want to get the work done in the morning and get home to watch on the television. There is just a little bit of urgency about the place. Any success means that going to work in the evening is that little bit easier. With Ragstone, there was a dinner in the banquet hall very soon after the race so the memory was still fresh. It was a long evening.

After that night, Ragstone was the most popular horse in Sussex. With just the 40 in the yard, Ragstone was the stable superstar. On the night of the dinner, the duke gave a speech. He had bad pins at the time. He said, "I've been walking round on my legs all day, but there was nothing wrong with them when I had to run down to the winner's enclosure to greet Ragstone." It meant everything to the duke, even though he was probably more into the cricket than horses. The win meant everything to the trainer too, so everything to us as well. We were all thrilled.'

Shirley Heights raised the bar again. 'We'd had runners in the Derby,' Wright recalls. 'Mount Athos, who finished third in 1968, was the first I remember. But Shirley Heights was the first one to have the town buzzing. To have a runner in the Derby who is fancied at 8–1? A lovely name too. Then, when he won, he was like a local celebrity. There was a party at the cricket pavilion for everyone. We just about left it standing.

'I rode him at two, then Rodney Boult – who ended up riding Desert Orchid for David Elsworth on the gallops – was on him at three. At the time, the older horses were first lot and the two-year-olds were second lot. For a year I rode Balmerino, who had won the New Zealand Derby before coming to England as a five-year-old and had real talent, then Shirley Heights. But the following year I had to give one of them up. In the end, the trainer decided I'd stay on Balmerino. That was fine with me. He was a known quantity with some really good form to his name. Shirley Heights? Well, he still had it all to prove.

'As a juvenile, Shirley Heights was very idle. I sat on him in the spring and you would never think that he'd make up into a Derby horse. He was bred to be a three-year-old and was very slow to come to hand at two. Just very idle. Lazy but also lively, and very fresh. He could whip round at any moment. But he wouldn't do anything like that actually on the gallops. A funny mix. I'm sure he dropped me a few times. He wouldn't be the only one! But he went on to be a Derby winner, so you'd be happy enough to accept being grounded every now and then. Likewise, if they go lazy at home and are fine at the track, that's fine. The lazy ones somehow always turn out to be the best. It is just the way they are.

'He stood out over the winter. He'd won as a two-year-old at Newmarket and won the Royal Lodge at Ascot, so we knew we had a nice horse. But nothing like, say, a Dewhurst winner who would be favourite for the Classics. Physically, he developed gradually. He was a good feeder. He would eat rocks, which helps. He was second in the Sandown Classic Trial. He blew up, up the hill. We knew he would be ahead the next time. The defeat was just laziness.'

A trip to Lady Herries' stable in West Sussex set up everything for the big day. 'With the good ones,' Wright continues, 'Mr Dunlop would take them for a racecourse gallop ten days or so before a big race, or take them over to Lady Herries. The point would be a change of scenery, to get them in the horsebox and with some different ground underfoot. Shirley Heights was a great traveller, one of those who would work better away from home. He needed to know that something special was occurring. He'd think, "Hey, this is a bit different! Something's up."'

When injury struck, Shirley Heights had already done enough at Epsom and the Curragh to take the yard up to another level. 'We knew that the setback he suffered was very serious. With a bowed tendon, it can be very bad. If the vet thought that the tendon was seriously damaged, that was it. Time and rest was all you could do. It happens in a big yard. These days, with us, we are lucky. There are always other horses coming along. The box isn't left empty. There is another one in there in no time.'

*

The arrival in Britain of the Maktoum family took the Dunlop stable to an even higher plane. Classic successes, like those of Salsabil, became the norm. 'I can remember Hatta, Sheikh Mohammed's first runner, who won a good few on the bounce,' Wright says. 'At the time I thought, "This is just another owner." I had no idea things would turn out the way they did. Who knows, if Hatta hadn't won a few races they might have gone into motor racing. At the time I just thought they were new owners who preferred evenings to mornings. You don't see the Maktoums on the gallops much. Sheikh Hamdan, who owned Salsabil, is a very good judge, though. He knows his pedigrees. He'd come down a couple of times a year and we'd stage a parade.

'Salsabil was always lovely-looking, but it was a

progression. You think, "Mmm, this could be a good one." Then you do a serious bit of work and you think, you know, "She's good." One step at a time, which is Mr Dunlop's way. Then they have to do it on the track – and she did that all right. She won her first race at Nottingham in September 1989 but got beaten a short head at Newbury two weeks later. Then, in October, she won the Prix Marcel Boussac at Longchamp in Paris. We knew she was good from day one, but the Boussac gives you different expectations. When she got beat at Newbury, Willie Carson wasn't that bothered. Back at the yard we were a bit disappointed, but he reassured us, said it was the ground – pretty firm. He was the man on top. He would know. He wasn't hard on her. He thought, "It's hard today; I'm not getting anywhere here." Then the ground came right in the Boussac. Looking back now, her defeat wasn't a setback. But at the time, watching on the television, it seemed to be. When Willie came in with his explanation it was a relief. But she had to redeem herself. We forgave her Newbury after Paris.

'She was sweet out on the gallops but could be a bit of a madam in the box at home. Not bad, though. She was a good feeder, but just a bit stroppy. The ears would go back, and she'd be a little precious at times. She wasn't straightforward. A little mean sometimes; a bit of a girl. If you wanted to do anything with her, like pull her mane, she would want to know what you wanted and why you were messing with her. But the good ones can have these little quirks. When the local television crews came to the yard,

I'm not sure if horses know they are being filmed, but she might have had an idea. She knew she was a star, for sure. Over winter she was developing all the time. She didn't spurt, but she did thrive, and then blossomed in the spring. A lot of fillies don't grow and develop. She really did. With her, there were expectations. If you win the Boussac then you are on the shortlist for Classic races. We certainly knew she was good, but they don't always do it.

'Circus Plume, our first Oaks winner, was quite similar in some ways. She was always a nice filly. She won her maiden at Salisbury then was third in the Fillies' Mile at Ascot. In 1984 she won three out of five, including the Oaks at Epsom, and the Oaks at York. As a two-year-old she started working well from about June. She was well bred. A little bit hyper at exercise, but she blossomed over the winter and progressed the right way. She was different to Salsabil in that she was never a madam. At worst she was a bit jig-joggy in the morning. Some of the good fillies can look a bit like colts but she was feminine enough and always meant business. She'd seem to think about things, but the good ones often tend to.

'The main difference between the Salsabil days and Circus Plume's time was the success in between. In the early days with Mr Dunlop, to have a runner in a big race was a thrill, but by the time of Salsabil we were a Group One stable. After the Boussac, our aim became the 1,000 Guineas. It wasn't a case of asking, "Is she a Classic filly?" We knew she should be. After the 1,000 Guineas we asked ourselves,

"Will she also be a Classic filly over a mile and a half?" Sheikh Hamdan wanted her to run over a mile and a half. Jockey and trainer knew she was top-class over a mile, and Mr Dunlop said after the Guineas that she might stay at a mile. The logic was, I think, she is better than any of the other filly milers the stable had had – better than Quick as Lightning, who won the 1,000 Guineas for us in 1980, and, looking back, better than Shadayid, who won the same race the year after Salsabil. Shadayid proved to be an out-and-out miler. She was out on her feet in the Oaks.'

Salsabil actually thrived over the extended trip. 'The saying goes, if they stay, they win,' Wright continues. 'In exercise on the gallops, you cannot tell. She had the pedigree to stay and the stats said she should stay. But there is always a question mark. We had our fingers crossed. We didn't work her over a mile and a half so there was a bit of a doubt. This made the Oaks more exciting. It helped that after the Guineas she began to mellow and settle down a bit. Looking back, the Guineas was probably her hardest race as a mile and a half was probably her best trip. After the Oaks, she was still in fine fettle. There isn't much time between the Oaks and the Irish Derby, but she was still thriving. It got a little bit easier for her as the season went on: the Oaks was a much easier race than the Guineas, and the Irish Derby was even easier. She could have run in the King George. She was certainly fresh enough to win it, and she was jumping out of her skin. But it was decided that we should save her for the Arc. A rest, then a trial, then Paris.

'With hindsight, I think maybe she peaked after the Irish Derby. It's hardly surprising as you cannot have them on that high for the whole season, especially when they are jumping out of their skin, which she was for July and a bit of August. After she had a rest, maybe she wasn't quite herself. But she didn't lose anything in never showing the same form again after winning in Ireland. She didn't sparkle in her trial – the Prix Vermeille – for the Arc. I remember at the time that the fear was she wasn't our Salsabil. I hadn't noticed in the days leading up to the race, but after her trial we had lower expectations. We had hoped she would hold her form, and she worked fine on the gallops. But it is at the track that matters. I remember afterwards talking about her in the yard. The word was, "That's it, then." But for those four races in the summer, she was special. They were great times, and you cannot expect much more from a filly. To have a runner in a Classic and win, to repeat that, and then to go on and take on the colts is the ultimate. Taking on the colts was bold.'

In terms of celebrating victories, times had moved on from the days of Shirley Heights and Ragstone. 'We didn't have formal parties for Salsabil like we did with Shirley Heights and Ragstone,' Wright recalls. 'We just made do on our own. By the time of Salsabil we were a Classic stable. We had a great time, sure, but races like the Guineas and Oaks were expected. We had a few drinks and were happy enough. A good few of the yard made a fair bit backing her over the winter at about 10–1. As for stories about odds of

25–1, some in the yard chased bigger prices but couldn't get on with any bookmakers. So much for inside information!'

*

Dunlop's second Derby winner, Erhaab, was less straight-forward than Shirley Heights. 'Erhaab ran six times at two and only won twice,' Wright says, 'so to go from that to winning the Derby was a real shock. I had canters on him and really didn't think he was anything special. No one in the yard had any expectations. The first inkling we got was at Newmarket when he finished second in the Feilden Stakes in his first start as a three-year-old. At the yard we didn't have any idea how good he would be. But after the race Willie Carson was over the moon. "He's all right, you know," he said.

'He was small, bonny, compact. But as for the Derby, riding him at two there was nothing to suggest what might come. If I am honest, nothing at all. He was bred to get a mile and a half and he showed a little bit of speed, which all Classic winners must have, but he kept coming back to the yard having been beaten. He started at Newmarket, then went to Newcastle and Leicester simply because we wanted at least to win with him, if only to help make him into a decent handicapper as a three-year-old and older. Over the winter he just blossomed, really flourished, and on the gallops he was going nicely enough, though never exceptionally. We weren't scratching our heads as he was getting better, and we have seen plenty who show a little on the gallops but don't reproduce it on the racecourse. Willie

Carson always said that he wanted further. He said that straight after Newmarket, which was over nine furlongs, and then he said the same after the Dante. You have to listen to him, as he was a very good judge. They win a race like that, three and a half lengths, easily and you don't want them stepping on stones. You don't want to pick up any virus that might be going round the yard either. Also, after Erhaab won the Dante there was the usual extra bit of security around the stable. That's for the public. They were backing him off the boards for the 1994 Derby with bookmakers. In such circumstances we would be sure that there was always someone watching him, sleeping in the yard. But every horse in the yard is a priority. Every horse is equal. But, as they say, some are more equal than others.

'With the Derby, the town gets involved, which is great for the yard. Like the Grand National, the race generates a big interest. When we have a runner, the folk in the town will have a shilling on him, and the local paper and Meridian TV come down, which adds to the buzz. In the Derby, Erhaab just flew, right at the point when the others began to slow down. Certainly he was the best horse in the race that day. Afterwards, we had our own party again. The Maktoum family is kind enough to make sure the yard is well rewarded. From their generosity, we make our own entertainment. You want to enjoy these moments. Everyone from the corn man – who'll be thinking, "The Derby winner ate my corn!" – to the vets. In the yard, we're all saying, "Hey, this is our boy!" I don't know whether you get that at

Newmarket. Here, in the town, we all enjoy a knock-on effect. Even the Arundel bookies enjoy a few days of feel-good. They may end up paying out a bit more than they are used to, but you still see them driving the Rolls-Royce!

'Whatever you say about how his Derby compares with other races, his name will still always be up there and his picture will still hang in the office at Arundel along with our other Derby winners. That day at Epsom was his day.'

*

Dunlop has been a constant in Wright's racing life. Likewise, for four decades, both Willie Carson and Pat Eddery. 'Jockeys didn't ride work for us as the boss wouldn't have them down,' Wright recalls. 'Lester Piggott took the ride on Circus Plume, but we never had him down here. Willie was a bit more welcome. He was a very good judge. When Willie said they had gears he was usually right, and he knew his pedigrees. He'd also pick them when they were too high in the weights, or not quite right. Willie had an answer to those who questioned the guv'nor's habit of working horses only on the all-weather before their debuts on grass. Willie would always say, "They are on grass when they are foals, aren't they?" A good answer. He was spot on with Bahri, too. When he finished third in the Guineas in 1995, you knew he would get better, and he was near his peak at Ascot in the autumn for the QEII. Then Willie took him under the trees for the good ground. He knew the track, the horse, and how to get the very best out of him.

'With Habibti, Willie would just say, "She's got gears." She was a lovely filly. Watching her on the gallops you would stand back. She liked her work. At home on the gallops, Habibti would leave her lead horse for dead. She wasn't asked to do that every time, but she always could. The first time Willie rode Habibti, he learnt what we all knew at home. We already knew she could go some. She was lovely at home, really straightforward. Sprinters can be like that. It can be a simple game, and she would just go in the direction you pointed her. Some fillies have quirks, that's for sure, but not her. She was uncomplicated at two, and at three when she finished horse of the year for 1983. She looked a sprinter from day one. We did try her over seven furlongs with the Guineas in mind, and no matter what work they do at home you only find out for sure on the track whether they stay. She didn't at all – simple as that.

'She had this rivalry with Soba, who was a very popular horse but pretty much always behind us. The north/south thing added to the sense of head-to-head. The town wouldn't be into this in the way that everyone took an interest in the Derby. Some folk would wonder a bit what all the fuss was about if we had a party to celebrate something like the Nunthorpe. But the stable was so proud of Habibti. She made the yard feel special. She was our girl. Looking back, she was probably one of the great sprinters, and for us the only really fast horse we have had up to now. She ran the sprinter's equivalent of the Guineas, Derby and King George. The programme was set out.'

As for Pat Eddery, he recorded winner number 4,000 on Silver Patriarch in the 1997 St Leger. 'Silver Patriarch was Pat's ride,' says Wright. 'He was a very lazy horse at home, and, to anyone who knew him well, on the track too. It would take Pat a while to get him going all right. We didn't know much about him until he won a two-year-old race at Newmarket over ten furlongs in November and Pat said how much he thought the horse had come on from the run before. But this was right at the end of the season. We weren't thinking about the Guineas or even the Derby, that's for sure. He wasn't particularly athletic, just lazy. That's even when he was walking. The public took to him because he was grey, and he was out the back before finishing like a train. This meant he was exciting to watch. But it was only because he didn't help the jockey early on. He was also taken a bit off his feet. In the Derby, if you remember, for most of the race he didn't seem to be going anywhere. Then he finished like a train.

'He was a lovely horse, kind to everyone. When I call him idle, maybe I really mean passive and laid back. He didn't seem to have a real competitive spirit. I don't know what he thought, but maybe life was passing him by a bit. He was better on Lady Herries' gallops. He certainly seemed to like a change of scenery. As an older horse, you noticed that he was still maturing. You knew he had an engine. With some extra maturity he'd only get better. The key then was just to keep him happy, make sure he was well fed, give him every chance.

'He won the Lingfield Trial, and that meant he was a live one for the Derby. Because he was grey the town was alight again, like it was for Shirley Heights. We were excited too, as he was a live chance and he'd shown he could come down the hill. In this respect he was athletic. Going into the Derby people worry less than you think about handling the course, as most will manage it once. In Silver Patriarch's case, he actually got better at managing the camber, which is why he then did well in the Coronation Cup, beating Swain, the following year. An intelligent horse like him is adaptable. He took it all in his stride, though he did only do just enough.

'After Epsom and just missing out on a Classic, we knew the extra two furlongs of the St Leger was perfect. A mile and a half was tough for him – the Coronation Cup at four over twelve furlongs meant he had his Group One, which was important commercially of course – whereas the extra distance came naturally. You could see that from the way he won races like the Geoffrey Freer at Newbury. Pat always said the extra distance was perfect for him. Looking back, all we had to do was keep him sound and the St Leger was his race. When he was running in the Irish Derby and at York in the Great Voltigeur, the feeling was always in the back of the mind, "Keep him right for the St Leger." He ran poorly in Ireland and we were all a bit concerned, as there seemed to be something wrong. In fact he had sort of gone back. In the end we realised that we had tried to make too much use of him, maybe to try and galvanise him. That wasn't for him.

'Pat also rode Millenary. Another old-timer. What can you say about him? His form is a book in itself. Physically he always looked the part, and, most important, he retained his engine season after season. At two we were hopeful, and he ran OK. At two we aren't disappointed if they don't win. We're not expecting too much from their first season. In some cases you know simply from their size that they won't win, and Millenary was a big, long, rangy horse. He was a good mover, though. From that we knew he could be good. We certainly never wrote him off as he had the frame, all right, he just had to fill out. After the winter there would be more to come.

'He won first time out at three, and the Chester Vase, then he got beat in bottomless ground at Chantilly in the French Derby. After that he got his act together properly in the Gordon Stakes and the St Leger. Because he was a nicely balanced horse, he could run anywhere. But he could be a bit grumpy in the box. His ears would go back, and he would always try and nip you. He had his own mind, but that is not a problem when they are that good. I'm sure he had a nip at me, but I've had plenty. Out of the box, it was a different story. On the gallops, today, fine, so long as there are not too many horses near him. He needs his space; I think he can feel a bit crowded. He'll pull a face when he's not happy. "Watch it" is what he's saying. He has got meaner with each season – the yard's grumpy old man. I'd say that we all suffer a bit from that.

'As horses grow older, you do always worry that they might lose their enthusiasm for the game or be slipping. Millenary won the Jockey Club Stakes as a four-year-old and was then second at five. You get a new kid on the block with allowances and all fresh to racing and you have to accept that. In his case there was no cause to panic. He'd follow the same pattern every season, pretty much. Yet, to be truthful, Millenary wasn't a good yardstick for other horses. He'd always prefer to do his own thing. Horses like Millenary, who stick around season after season, stay with you, especially if you ride them. He's the gaffer. He makes sure we know. If they do stick around, you cannot help but become attached to them. In my case, Captain Horatius was a real favourite. He'd lead the good ones as he was just a bit keen in a canter. I just loved him. He wasn't a top horse, but he was a nice horse. Rode him for six years, until he was eight. He won about ten races in his own right, but that isn't all that important.

'The box ride to Lady Herries' yard and the gallop there and sweat – all that helps to keep an older horse like Millenary fresh. After a trip to Lady Herries', usually ten days before a big race, he'd know that he has done more than he usually does at home, and that something at the racecourse is coming up. Lady Herries' is a pretty stiff gallop. Only the naughty ones who are unruly at home don't react favourably. But that is how they are, everywhere.'

*

Every stable has its ups and downs, and the occasional Chilibang. Wright credits Dunlop with keeping everything on an even keel. 'Mr Dunlop always keeps it simple. An honourable, professional man. I have just lived off the back of his success. He is still so full of enthusiasm. He's very good if there is a problem, and he's a great organiser. What are we going to do about this? Do this and do that. No ums and ahs. He has a natural way for organising, not just for racing. He is always immaculately dressed and in control. It helps that we are private stables. We are up on the hill, above the town. With this, and the boss's organisation, everything is very calming. Plus we have the gallops to ourselves so we don't have to rush for a strip of ground like they do in Newmarket and other training centres. He is always on a level. Good morning, how are things, need to sort this out, sort that out. Always calm. He's not always in a suit. He has his work clobber and gear. But he'd be smart in a pair of wellies. What you see is what he is. Like the rest of us he enjoys the highs but he also accepts the lows. Either way, he wants to get on. After a defeat, he'll ask, "What wins tomorrow?"'

Chilibang often posed questions. 'With Chilibang – at four, in 1988, he won the King's Stand Stakes at Royal Ascot – you never really knew what was round the corner. He was a bit quirky, especially at home. An absolute angel at the racecourse, and in his stable, but on the gallops a real handful. As a two-year-old he won five times thanks to some good placing by the trainer. Then at three he picked up a listed race at Newmarket, which showed clearly that he had talent. But for some reason between three and four he turned into a real bull of a horse. He became very bossy, and after a winter of just trotting he was quite hard to handle. He didn't want to do anything fast at all, from walking to working on the gallops. In fact he could be very difficult to get on the gallops at all. On work days we had to lead him on to the gallops. One day we even needed a van behind him so we could toot the horn and bang the doors shut. He went, eventually.

'I had my scares with him. Once, he was being led to the gallops as usual and he spooked. The fellow holding the lead rein lost his grip so Chilibang was able to bolt up the gallops with the loose leather flapping around between his legs. It could have been a disaster. Blinkers helped most of the time, but he was still stroppy, digging in his feet. After a gallop one day we went grazing, just to pick at some grass. It was hot and he always made me work, so I undid the zip of my jacket. At the same time his head went down and I was over the top, landing on all fours. I heard the other riders shouting. He took a chunk out of my shoulder and ripped the jacket off in the process. After that we put on a muzzle. Willie Carson never knew what he was like at home. His breeches would have been brown if he had. Once you have put a muzzle on them there is nowhere else to go. At two he just got on with it, and at three, but at four he'd got wise to the game. It meant that 1988 was a long summer for me.'

There have been a few of those, mostly good ones, for Wright, down by the sea.

CHAPTER FIVE
CORKY BROWNE

Fred Winter, Nicky Henderson,
Cheltenham and Aintree

Life would have been very different for Corky Browne had he been able to reach Newbury during the harsh winter of 1963. A young Irishman with experience of riding as an apprentice on the Flat, he'd travelled to Lambourn in search of daily racing instead of just twice a week back home. 'No racing for six weeks when I arrived in the village,' he recalls. 'I was a new boy. They were delivering eggs, milk and bread by helicopter. I thought, "They said the weather was bad in Ireland." If I could have made it out of Lambourn, I'd have headed off home.'

On reflection, Browne is glad he didn't perform a spectacular U-turn. Today he can look back on a career of over 40 years at the highest level. With Fred Winter he shared in the success of two Grand National winners in a row: first Jay Trump in 1965, then Anglo the following year. With Nicky Henderson, there was a triple Champion Hurdle winner in See You Then. To follow that was one of the best Queen Mother Champion Chase winners there's been, in Remittance Man. Accompanied, of course, by his loyal friend Nobby the sheep. In addition, Browne has witnessed some of the game's best riding talent mature into the finished article. One of the best was John Francome. Browne remembers a green kid, just sixteen, straight from international show jumping. 'He got too close to the fences,' the guv'nor told him. Very amateur with the stick too, Browne adds with a laugh. 'At the beginning, desperate. Wish I'd had a camera. But by God he came good.'

Some progress for Browne along the way too. Not long ago he made the last mortgage payment on his Lambourn home. One way or another, he eventually just about made racing's system of rewards work. The going rates for stable staff in the 1960s and 1970s drove him out of the game for a while. After ten years working with Winter he wasn't earning anywhere near enough to support a new wife and young family. Alternative employment – painting and decorating – for three years gave him a chance of establishing a foothold in the property market. The work was also easier on Browne's back, which he had injured in a fall as a teenager back home.

Browne might still be up a ladder now had he not been asked by the Flat trainer Roger Charlton to give his then Windsor House home a fresh coat. Ahead of taking out a licence, Charlton had set up an equine swimming-pool business. Browne was on hand to pull the boss out the day he fell in. For his rescue efforts, he landed himself the manager's job on money that was an improvement on the £29 a week which was his last pay cheque at Fred Winter's yard. When Nicky Henderson came calling, on Winter's recommendation, looking for a head lad, Browne returned to the jumping fold once a comparable package had been negotiated.

While he was out of racing, Browne reckons that he 'realised every morning' what he was missing. In his case, that meant no more highs like those provided by Bula, Lanzarote and Pendil, who delivered Champion Hurdle and King George honours for the yard. Once he was back in the game, with Henderson, there were nearly 30 other Cheltenham winners. Marlborough won the National Hunt Chase in 2000; Bacchanal was successful in the Stayers' Hurdle that same year. As well as great days there have been the inevitable downs. Fred Winter's Killiney, talented enough as a novice chaser to feature as third favourite in the Gold Cup betting, smashed his shoulder. An injury to Bacchanal's hock proved fatal. 'Jumping's the greatest game in the world, but you still see bad legs,' Browne accepts. Knee surgery has reinforced Browne's own pins, which are good for a few more years yet.

A belated great escape to Newbury for a ride home is the furthest thought from Browne's mind in his fifth decade of racing. 'New stock comes into the yard and makes you think that there are going be some winners,' he says. 'Another good one arrives – that's what it's all about. Young ones are coming in every year, so how can you retire?' With

Henderson's help, Browne should avoid the mistake of quitting prematurely. 'The guv'nor said he won't let me,' he jokes. Nor is there good reason to encourage such a devoted man into hasty retirement. 'I worry about things when I am away from the yard,' he confesses. 'I'll put bandages on one of them and leave for the evening. Then, at eleven p.m., I'll be thinking, "Maybe the bandages are too tight." That's the worst thing you can do. My wife says, "You've done all you can." But I still come back and check sometimes to be sure.'

*

Browne was part of an Aintree-winning yard within a year of arriving in Britain. Twelve months later he went to Aintree in person, to saddle Anglo. 'Anglo and Jay Trump were very different,' says Browne. 'Anglo was a small, flashy chestnut with four white socks and a face. Like a Flat horse – 15.3 maybe. People would say he was sixteen, but he wasn't. Jay Trump was a nice big horse, a Christian to ride, and a good jumper. With the National in mind, Mr Winter would build up a fence in the back paddock to give them some idea of what they would face on the day. The fences in those days were a tremendous challenge.' With Jay Trump, the jockey needed some fine-tuning too. 'Tommy Smith had to lose some weight. He was a big man – over twelve stone. Mr Winter got him on a bicycle so that he would ride to work instead of driving. He'd cycle down from Upper Lambourn. Losing the weight wasn't easy for him. He had to cut back on his socialising. You wouldn't put money on everything he rode. For me, that would be true of most amateurs. But in this case he really knew the horse. That was his advantage. And that he was a horseman.

'We watched the race on television, an old black-and-white set. We all gathered round. One of us watching was urging on Jay Trump. In all the excitement we knocked the television off the desk. We all just moved forward and carried on watching, with the telly smoking away on the floor. One fellow in the yard had a Mini. There were seven of us. We all went round the village in this car sounding the horn, up the high street. When we eventually got back to the yard, the television was still lying on the floor.'

Extra effort on Anglo throughout the following year paid dividends all round. 'He was a great ride,' says Browne, 'except when he was a lazy bugger. The guv'nor got a suit out of his National. Ryan Price was Anglo's first trainer. He didn't think he would make it round Aintree. He had a side bet with Mr Winter. Anglo wasn't the best of jumpers. He would test every fence and did so in his last run before the National. More of a park horse. But he got round when it mattered, so the guv'nor got his suit. For me, the best thing about riding Anglo and looking after him was that I got to Aintree. When I was at home in Ireland I always wanted to see the fences. I may not be that tall, but I have seen big men stand by them and be dwarfed. I wanted a simple souvenir of the place.

'I had to think again when he won the race. To lead up one there was a good thing; to lead up the winner was another thing altogether. I ran out to meet him just after he passed the winning post. I grabbed him and he almost carried me along off the floor. If I had arrived any earlier I might have made him duck out before the finish line. I was going ballistic. He had his ears pricked at the line and was still going strong, so he just lifted me up round his neck. Tim Norman, who rode him – he had a car crash the week before the race – kept saying, "Let him breathe, will you!" When we got back to the yard, a big bedsheet was on the wall of the house: Welcome Home Mighty Anglo! He was 50–1, and I had £20 on him. I forgot to collect the money on the day. I remembered about that later, for sure.'

Killiney, on the other hand, left Browne thinking what might have been. 'To look after Anglo was great,' he recalls. 'He was a grand horse. But to have a horse like Killiney? Well, he was the best horse I have ever seen. A mighty one on the gallops – 17.2 hands – and no trouble at all around the yard. Frightening at times. Not to ride him, you know – that was great. But frightening to think that he could drop you and then a once-in-a-lifetime horse would be loose. You'd worry what might go wrong when you were up. And when he was fresh he could be a lively bugger. He could pull some on the gallops. You couldn't school anything with him. It is normally best that you school horses together so that in a race, when they are jumping, they're used to seeing another horse alongside. He had to be schooled on his own. You couldn't settle him and he just wanted to get on with it. That was no good for any that schooled with him. In that respect, he was a bit brainless. He once took off nineteen feet outside the wing. Fred Winter measured it. That is not thinking. Maybe if he had survived longer he would have learnt.'

It ended as a tragic story of unfulfilled potential. 'Eight out of eight as a novice was something,' Browne continues. 'I don't remember a winning distance less than 25 lengths. When he won the SunAlliance at Cheltenham in 1973, it was a job to pull him up. As a novice he worked with Pendil – Richard Pitman rode – and Bula. Good horses can work together no matter whether they race over hurdles or fences. In his case there wasn't a novice good enough to stay with him. The guv'nor said to me, "Sit in behind, and don't you dare head them. Start behind them and finish behind them. You can hold him, you know him, you have always known him. So get on with it." At the time I was a bit green and brainless myself. I'd tend to work horses more so I'd know personally what they were capable of. Like in a fast car – you want to find out the maximum speed. Even after the guv'nor's warning, that day I did my very best to hold him, but he still left them. I got a right bollocking for that. I deserved a few, but I couldn't help that one. I had a bad back from a fall in Ireland, and riding Killiney just made it worse. I'd ride with my irons as short as Lester Piggott, trying to hang on. The sad thing is that he should have proved how good he really was on the racecourse.

'He had nearly a season off after hurting his hock. Mr Winter gave him the whole year to rest up. The vets reckoned four months, so Mr Winter thought, "Not enough time to prepare for Cheltenham. In a year off he'll hopefully strengthen up." The next season when he came in again, I thought, "Blimey. It was a struggle to hold him before; how am I going to manage it now?" He was huge.'

Then came the fateful day. 'You always think today might be the race,' says Browne. 'Killiney's was the Heinz Chase at Ascot in April 1973. It was the first time I took my wife racing. Another horse made the running in the race. The guv'nor had told Richard Pitman, who rode him, to tuck in behind. The other horse took off too soon and landed in the ditch. Killiney, a much better jumper, was coming from further back and he hit the fence hard. He got his foot caught and that broke his shoulder. He realised in mid-air. You could have folded his leg up it was so badly broken. I came home in the car instead of the horsebox. I didn't want to see anyone or anything to do with the horse after that, especially the empty box. That evening, Mr Winter came round my house with a bottle of brandy. He asked my wife, "How is he?" She said, "He isn't speaking." We drank the brandy together. Didn't touch the sides, if I remember. Not even a kick out of it. He said, "You can come back tomorrow, if you want, or next month, if you want, or come back next year. I know what you are feeling. Me? Today, I've lost one of the best horses I have ever trained. But you won't do much good moping round the house." After he'd gone I went out for a walk, went down the pub. There was a fellow there who had been giving me some trouble. I said to him,

"I've heard you say you could take me. How about now?"
So I thumped him and we had a scrap. The next morning I
went back to work. But not Killiney's old box. I couldn't go
near it.'

*

See You Then was the breakthrough horse for the
partnership of Nicky Henderson and Corky Browne. He
was a challenge from the start. 'There was only just under a
fortnight between him arriving and the Triumph Hurdle,'
Browne recalls. 'He was nasty. We put a Yorkshire boot on
him within five days. It took us three days to take it off.
Worked around him the best way we could, without being
bitten. In the stable it was tricky; outside he was fine. He
knew the guv'nor's voice. But he didn't really like him! He
was just fidgety. He'd squeeze you against the wall. We all
had holes in our jumpers from where he had taken a nip.
Luckily, he did mellow. By the end I could bandage him up
loose. He was actually worse tied up in his later years. We
all mellow over time. At least that's what people say.'

The extra hours on the gallops made the difference. 'He
certainly was the breakthrough horse for us,' says Browne,
'the first one we knew had a chance of something big like a
Champion Hurdle. You still have to believe it. You don't
grasp it until it happens, until the guv'nor's walking across
the parade ring towards you with tears in his eyes. After See
You Then's first in 1985, I just grabbed him. See You Then
was always brilliant schooling, electric over hurdles. When

a horse can jump that quick then that's three-quarters of it. He was just a natural. Jumping at Cheltenham, if you miss one out you have no chance of getting back into the race.

'He always had three bad legs and one good one. The front legs were not good – horrible, really. After the Triumph Hurdle he went to Italy for their version of the race. He won that very easily but he did come back with his problems. He looked a bit sore. We blistered them in those days, which helped. He'd be fresh without the exercise. When he was recuperating, you had to keep your eye out for him. After the races he was better, a bit more relaxed. He knew he had done well. But he was like every great sporting star: he had a thing about him. Like a boxer, or a footballer. The good ones have a sting in them.'

The seasons took their toll, though. 'With each Champion Hurdle, it did become more stressful,' Browne concedes. 'We were expected to win, which is different. I'd be a bit snappy in the mornings leading up to the Cheltenham Festival, on Saturday when he worked and before he was due to run. By the third Champion Hurdle in 1987 we were struggling to keep him going. The greatest anxiety was always a couple of months before Cheltenham. With him, the timing of everything was crucial. The first run was always a case of him just coming back fine. Didn't matter where he finished as long as he was sound the following morning. He wasn't running for that race, it was just prep for Cheltenham, and for that the fresher he was the better. It could be touch and go if the weather was bad. One year we just managed to squeeze a race into him in time by going to Haydock. We would have to go to the beach with him, everywhere on the Downs, on any gallop or racecourse, just to keep him on schedule. With his legs you had to find good ground. The swimming-pool was also essential – the one at Windsor House where I had worked after leaving Mr Winter. He was a natural. Luckily, he took to it straight away.

'I went to Cheltenham every time for his Champion Hurdles. I'd do my morning's work at the yard, then head for the course – about an hour's journey – so I'd be able to put the bandages on him. I'd watch the race miles away from the track. I'd just walk around, around, around. The people with me would say, "Why don't we go and look at the shops or something?" They were the last thing on my mind. I made sure I didn't get there too early. The later I got there the better. Worse than the guv'nor.'

See You Then set a mark for the yard, and the likes of Remittance Man maintained the standard, and met growing expectations. 'When we had a few winners on the board, Cheltenham was that bit more serious for the stable,' Browne recalls. 'After Remittance Man won the Arkle in 1991, next year the Champion Chase was there to win. We couldn't sit back too much and enjoy the moment.

'Remittance Man was a terrible box walker for the first couple of months. He was returnable – we'd bought him at the sales – and I think the guv'nor thought about it. We tried tyres hanging in the box, bales of hay, but he just weaved his way around them. Then we tried different sheep. Ridley was the first – had to be Ridley, really. Then an Alan. We struck lucky with Nobby. Remittance Man seemed to like him. Then, for some reason, he was changed. We had to fetch him back because they missed each other. When Remittance Man went out in the morning, Nobby would be making all sorts of noises. They had to go racing together as well. But feeding Remittance Man was the hardest. There was nothing on him. I had to feed him little and often. That way he got used to it. He had his quirks, but all the good ones have something about them.

'He was very moderate over hurdles, and not much of a work horse. He did at least win his bumper. He got beaten at Newton Abbot on Boxing Day 1988. Nothing to shout about. Certainly not good enough to become what he did within two years. The guv'nor thought about running him over three miles as a hurdler. We didn't know what to do to get the best out of him. In the end, the fences made him. When we first schooled him, we thought, "Crikey, he jumps. He'll win his novice all right. He'll make a chaser." At Cheltenham he would make up lengths at each jump. He certainly did in both the Arkle and the Champion Chase. There could have been even more, elsewhere. He'd have won a King George in 1991 had he been better ridden by Jamie Osborne. Nothing in that race to take him on. He hit the front five from home. Would never have happened if Richard Dunwoody had been riding. But he was on Desert Orchid. Richard would have waited longer. The best jockey of them all, including Tony McCoy. Gained lengths coming away from the fences, and great at reading a race too.

'Remittance Man fell in the Champion Chase of 1994. That should have been Travado's to win. He could certainly go a bit on the gallops. Early on in his career he won the Arkle, and you might have thought he was going to finish better than Remittance Man. Never quite that good, though. In the Champion Chase after Remittance Man fell, Travado was taken to the outside. He was one that you just left alone to jump. In the end, not quite good enough on the day. He was a big horse, bigger than Remittance Man, but not better. Few are.'

*

The very best achieve greatness. The very good, like Marlborough and Bacchanal, must make the most of what chances they get. 'Marlborough's year for winning the Gold Cup was 2001, which saw the foot and mouth outbreak when they had to cancel Cheltenham,' Browne rues. 'He was at his best then. Looking back, you could see that he had a real chance. After that there was Best Mate. That was it as far as Gold Cups were concerned for him. But we really fancied Bacchanal for the Gold Cup in 2002. He was never 100 per cent in his back, which had always caused him a few problems, but for Cheltenham that year he was spot on. It was terrible, the following year, when he smashed his fetlock at the same course.

'Marlborough was always a funny jumper. He was a

good old horse, but he would make those bad blunders. If he met the fence wrong, he couldn't get out of it. The trick was keeping him up with the pace. Even then he could make those big mistakes. Schooling – you had to make him do it. He wasn't a natural at all. Mick Fitzgerald, our stable jockey, spent a lot of time just trying to work him out. He schooled him a lot with a good few horses. He had some horrific falls. Mick learnt that there was always that chance. No little mistakes, just big ones.

'Bacchanal went smoothly from hurdles to fences. The back was always a problem, but we hoped that the fences would make him think more. He was schooled a lot, and he took a while, but he got it right in the end. A very good-natured horse. When he was injured at Cheltenham in the Pillar Chase they brought him back to the racecourse stables in an ambulance. We had a look. I thought, "No chance." It was bad. I thought, "We could spend a lot of time with him and the result would be no different." The owners arrived. It was their call. I said, "It's very bad." The guv'nor said, "If it was mine . . ." Then he said to me, "Can you hold him?" It is the worst part of racing, the wrong side of the game, but it has to be done. Any injury to a good horse is horrible. Not just for your own yard but for everyone. When Best Mate missed the Gold Cup, no one would be happy about that. Can happen to Flat horses too, not just jumpers. But Flat racing is the easiest game in the world. They come back from racing without a scratch, nothing. Everything fine. They could all run the next day.'

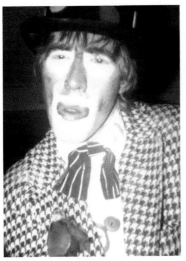

*John Joyce at Henry Cecil's
Christmas party*

*John Joyce at Jack Hanson's
stable*

John Joyce at work today [© Arnhel de Serra]

Above and left: *Joyce Wallsgrove with Early Spring [© J& C Racing Pictures, Provincial Press Agency]*

Larry Poland with Hallo Dandy

Larry Poland today [© Arnhel de Serra]

Above: *Dennis Wright on Balmerino*

Left: *Dennis Wright at John Dunlop's yard, February 2004*

Above: *Dennis Wright on Chilibang*

Right: *Corky Browne at Seven Barrows, January 2004*

Gerry McCann at Kingwood Stables, June 2004 [© Matthew Faber]

Gerry McCann with Nashwan

Gerry McCann (right) heading home.

Above: *Jimmy Scott*
Left: *Stuart Messenger with Kribensis,
February 2004 [© Chris Bourchier]*

Below: *Jimmy Scott with Kieren Fallon*

Top: *Lisa Jackson (left) on Flagship Uberalles (along with Village King)*

Middle: *Lisa Jackson smiling at Flagship Uberalles*

Right: *Lisa Jackson on Clifton Beat*

Left: *Ian Willows at Bedford House, Newmarket, June 2004*

Left: *Ian Willows in 1963 [© R Anscombe]*

Below: *Ian Willows (right) at Newmarket in 1975*

Above: *Rodney Boult with Desert Orchid, February 2004 [© John Beasley]*

Above right: *Rodney Boult leading out 'Dessie'*

Right: *Rodney Boult as a teenager*

Below: *Rodney Boult at Ascot [© David Hastings Photographs]*

*

Nicky Henderson and Fred Winter – Browne has never worked for any other trainer. 'At Fred Winter's,' he recalls, 'we did what we could to entertain ourselves. It could be boring, for sure. We made our own sort of fun. There were no wine bars and discos. There was the Legion in the village, but most in there were a bit old. We'd cycle to Swindon or Newbury. We'd race: next to the third telegraph pole wins. We'd go to the pictures or a dance. And there were plenty of pranks, as you can imagine. The lads would play a trick with a broom handle which they'd wedge under the knob of your door to keep you in your room. During the six-week freeze of 1963 I woke up one morning and I couldn't get out. I thought, "They've done me." So I climbed through a window. I remembered then that there was snow outside. You couldn't see across the yard. They made a gap in the snow up the main street. If you met a car coming down, you had to reverse. And when it melted, that was worse.

'The guv'nor taught me my first lesson during this time. They had carved another route through the snow so we could walk the horses. The guv'nor asked me to walk one straight down. He swerved left and right, hitting the sides of snow. The guv'nor came over. "Give him here," he said. He kept one hand up by the ears and pulled the other one right down one side of the horse's face. Walked in a perfect straight line for him.

'Mr Winter never went that ballistic or screamed. One morning I was due to ride one of two as a pair. He said to

129

me, "I want you to lead off and stay together so that you finish together." Of course me, brainless, I had to win the gallop. So I finished a few lengths ahead. Back then I didn't know that no race is won on the gallops. When we all finished riding work, the guv'nor came over to me. "How did he go? He seemed to go well?" "Yes, guv'nor," I said, "he did." "Better than the other horse?" the guv'nor asked. "Yes," I said, "a stone better." He said, "As far as I remember, did I ask you to finish together?" "Yes, guv'nor." "So, was there a reason you finished ahead of the other horse? I'd just like to know, you understand." I'd have preferred a bollocking to this. So I said, "The other horse couldn't go with me." The guv'nor paused. "You know," he said, "I thought the other horse might be able to go with you. I was wrong about that. But the reason you were together was for your horse to bring the other on and not disappoint him. Which is what you have just done. If he couldn't go with you, you should have stayed with him. Now he's fed up with racing. Instead of being able to go with your horse maybe next week – because I promise you he is good enough if he has the confidence – it is going to take longer. You could have helped him. Try and listen to what I am saying in future, would you?" A smack in the face or a kick in the arse – either would have been preferable to that conversation. I felt tiny; it was stupid of me. The guv'nor would leave you to think about what you'd done all day. Every day, Mr Winter made me think. I thank him for that now.'

Nicky Henderson had been Winter's amateur jockey and assistant for five years. Then he started training himself, and for that he needed staff. 'Mr Winter would send me a Christmas card,' Browne says of his time spent away from the game decorating for some much-needed cash, 'and every week I would see him at church. One Sunday he asked me, "Did you take that job with Nicky Henderson?" He'd come knocking when he was going to start training. I hadn't let him in the house at first. I said, "You don't even know me. Have any of Fred Winter's lads – the best in the land, in the world." "Hear me out," he said. Mr Winter had said that he could take any lad for the job but didn't think any of them were right for head lad, except me. I was someone who had left the game because he had a wife and two kids to support. He respected that but he'd been sad to lose me. I said, "Mr Henderson, I got out of racing years ago. The game doesn't pay. Simple as that. I do still miss it, but not as bad as I did." To be truthful, I couldn't remember Nicky's first name. At Mr Winter's he had been the stable amateur. Me? Back then, I wasn't going to take any amateur seriously. We were riding out one day and I said to him, "You lie up and I'll wait for you." "Who do you think you are?" he said to me. "I'll let you know when you finally make it to the top of the hill," I said, and was off.

'The guv'nor said to me, "Write down on a piece of paper what you want pay-wise, and drop round the note in an envelope." Right there, I said, "I'm not going to earn less than what I am making painting and decorating." He came back two days later, after I had delivered the envelope. "This is ridiculous,' he complained. "No one could afford this. Could you come down?" I said I wasn't doing it for less, and I wanted a £10 rise every year whatever the rise the rest negotiated. He said, "I'll think about it." I said, "There are lads half the price up the road that would be grand." He came back later that week. "OK," I said. "Put it all down on paper. You write better than I do. I'll see you Monday morning." It was a challenge. I was one of the lads at Mr Winter's, but now I had a job. You can't be one of the gang. You can't let anyone down.'

*

Corky Browne mainly looks ahead. Only occasionally does he cast a glance back to the great days. 'I watched Crisp's second in the 1973 Grand National the other day. Still a pain. If Richard Pitman – he did improve over the years as a jockey – had left his stick down he would have won the race. Couldn't use his stick at the best of times. A great horse – Red Rum, of course – beat him, but that doesn't make things any better. Maybe if Crisp had been held up and had come through, just got beat on the line, it might be easier to accept now. A big, lean, bonny horse, tall – 16.2 hands, maybe 16.3. When Crisp arrived at Mr Winter's from Australia he had bones sticking out of him. When they come from there it is often the wrong part of the year for them. Still, he was a natural jumper. Took to that straight away.

'Pendil? He didn't look top-class at first, but when he

went chasing you could see his talent. Bula? He was big and backward. Nobody wanted to look after him. A goat; a leg in four different counties for his first year. Big, clumsy Bula – never looked a Champion Hurdler! When Stan Mellor rode him the guv'nor said, "Not the best jumper; don't take any chances." Flattened the last two hurdles completely. Stan came back afterwards. "The best novice I've ever ridden," he said. I backed the favourite – against Bula! – in the race. Couldn't believe I lost my money. Proved to be the best novice ever. A machine inside, the guv'nor reckoned. Lanzarote was a different type altogether. A really good-looking horse – more upright, a bit more classy, classical. We worked on Bula's jumping. He could always make those big mistakes. Paul Kelleway would have him out the back, last of 30 with two furlongs to go, and crucify him to get up by a head. Luckily, Bula was tough. He carried the weight, which proved how special he was. Third in the Gold Cup behind Ten Up, before the mare Dawn Run won it eleven years later in 1986. Only the ground beat us that day. Took to fences better, I think, than the guv'nor thought he would. You don't get ground like we did for Cheltenham in 1975 these days. Nor the winters of old.'

Times have changed in other ways. 'There was a lot more steady work in the early days,' Browne recalls. 'They've cut down on that now. More on the all-weather, less road work, lots of trotting. Work is over a shorter distance. You go up the all-weather once, twice, three times, rather than a mile, mile and a quarter. Horses are also more handled when they are young so they are better behaved when they come to us. In the past, horses would last six, seven years. Not many do these days. They come from France and Germany rather than Ireland. There aren't many like Marlborough and others we've been lucky to have. Horses like him come to the yard and straight away you think, "The Gold Cup, the Hennessy."'

Still, there is always something new to learn. 'When Barry and John Hills went off to America, I asked them, "Can you bring back some tapes of the way they bandage the legs there?" Horses racing at that pace on that surface on those tight tracks? Well, they must be well bandaged, mustn't they?'

Cheltenham remains the goal for Corky Browne over 40 years on. 'Nothing beats that winner's enclosure and the feeling you get from being in it,' he says enthusiastically.

CHAPTER SIX
GERRY McCANN

Major Hern, Nashwan,
Royal Standards

Gerry McCann hasn't had many job interviews during a career that stretches back to the 1960s. In 1973 references from Bill Wightman were good enough for the late Dick Hern. Marcus Tregoning, the Major's successor when he retired in 1997, had seen more than enough during his days as Hern's assistant. The consensus has been that McCann, who is chairman of the Stable Lads' Association, was right to skip America. After serving his apprenticeship with Wightman, the plan was to head home to Ireland for rides then hit America with winners under the belt. Instead, Mac, as Hern called him, took his work saddle to West Ilsley.

Today, McCann is comfortably resident at Tregoning's Kingwood stables, to where Hern relocated in 1990 after the Queen did not renew his lease for West Ilsley. As well as Kingwood, McCann's other home is Lambourn's Wheelwright Arms. He hasn't fallen into bad habits ahead of his retirement: he and his brother Sean are a third of the way through their fifteen-year lease on the pub. 'My pension,' he jokes.

The retirement fund has been handsomely boosted over the years by some good-priced successes. There were the Derby winners McCann helped prime for Epsom: Troy, brave Henbit and Nashwan, who obliged, respectively, at ante-post odds of 40–1, 20–1 and 33–1. Henbit defied a cracked cannon bone in the home straight to deliver for the stable. With Dayjur, champion sprinter, it wasn't so much the opportunity to make a few quid but the chance to be associated with greatness. McCann still shakes his head at the colt's turn of foot, and his flying leap at the death in the Breeders' Cup Sprint with the race as good as won. With fillies, McCann simply dealt with the very best, and the prestige of the Queen's dual Classic winner Dunfermline. Sun Princess, Bireme and Height of Fashion were show stoppers. And add to the colts' list the last-named's sons, Unfuwain and Nayef, as well as the incomparable Nashwan, McCann's number one ride of them all.

The unpredictable nature of horse talent like Nashwan's deep reserves still holds McCann's attention. He remembers how Hern would do his best to assess potential. 'The Major would never go overboard, but he had a real eye for a horse. He'd be right most times, but not always. Sometimes he'd say, "That might be my Derby horse," and the lads would be laughing away about it. You'd say, "That's nice. I just hope he has an engine." It's all about the way they develop. You have an ordinary two-year-old, then, over the winter, the colt or filly becomes Classic standard at three. You see them change.'

Some, like Nashwan's half-brothers Unfuwain and Nayef, can take time. The hands of Unfuwain's devoted groom were singed by the bookmakers after a debut defeat. Belief in the colt's talent had advanced ahead of nature's progress. McCann and co. left some bandages in the colt's box with a note explaining that they were for their colleague's 'burnt fingers'. The defeat of Bustino, whom McCann helped prepare for the 'race of the century' against Grundy, was a shared reversal. The whole yard backed the stable's colt to win the King George VI and Queen Elizabeth Stakes of 1975. However, Bustino's owner, Lady Beaverbrook, was well known for softening such financial blows with some comfortingly crisp notes. Hern's other patrons were a contrast. Dick Hollingsworth was racing's own version of Howard Hughes – never seen at the yard. The Queen was the opposite and often mucked in on her regular visits.

In the saddle, you learn the insight that every owner craves about his or her investment, McCann maintains. 'From there you could sometimes tell more than the Major, or any trainer. You feel the adrenalin. Like in a big car when you put your foot down and you shift back in the seat. You are driving along the motorway in a Ferrari doing 70mph and you know that there is more under the bonnet than that.' When they come in as yearlings, you can't say, McCann insists. For this conclusion he is drawing on his 40-plus years in the game. 'All horses have different aspects – a good walker, a great looker,' he says. 'But even so, in the end on the gallops and at the racecourse maybe they are just no good. You can never tell, really. It is like a kid who walks into the boxing gym. Look how scrawny he is – what is he doing here? That one can turn out to be the best fighter around.'

*

Troy and Henbit were back-to-back Derby winners for the yard, in 1979 and 1980 respectively. Henbit was McCann's ride at both two and three. With Troy he helped make sure that this bull of a horse was exercised hard enough to keep the weight off his legs. 'Riding Henbit, underneath I always knew that there was more to come,' reckons McCann. 'We always knew that he was good. As for a Derby winner? At two, and into the spring at three, I wasn't so sure. In the end, a surprise to everyone, if I am honest. In the trials he was workmanlike, nothing special. Then two weeks before the Derby he suddenly thrived. You'd have said at that point, "This one is the Derby winner." In May he just changed into a champion. You could have picked him out of 40 horses. He just stood out. I'd been riding him, but even I didn't know until two weeks before Epsom. The Major brought him on physically to be at his peak then. We all knew that he was the business from his appearance. Under the Major, he thrived. He just ceased to be simply one of the string.'

There were similarities between Troy and Henbit. 'Both had engines,' McCann says. 'Troy progressed through his three-year-old season. He got bigger and stronger. Problem was he also became much heavier. This meant that we had to work him more and more. He was simply getting too big for his legs. It was tricky. He had to have the extra work to keep the weight off. He'd work, and work, and work, at least twice a week and half speed just on the way to the gallops. Without this he'd have broken down. His legs wouldn't have been able to carry him. As well as keep the weight off, we had to keep him fresh. It was a balancing act. Troy was beaten as a two-year-old at Salisbury, which the Major liked because it was fair and a good, galloping track. To be honest, I could not believe the result. I think he was beaten by one of Barry Hills' yard, Nobloys, and I don't remember that one ever winning another race, whatever his name was. We all still thought he was a good horse, though. In Troy's races at two, Willie Carson looked after him. He always did with ours. The consensus was that Troy would be a much better horse over twelve furlongs at three. From his attitude and the way he went about things we knew he was good. He knew he was too. He was also very powerful, very athletic.

'Troy would never have won the Guineas, not even a bad one. I backed him for the Derby at 40–1 after he won the Sandown Classic Trial. The race wasn't televised that year for some reason. A friend of mine rang from the track and said that Troy had won narrowly. "How good is this Troy?" he asked me. I said it sounded disappointing. My friend answered that if I had seen the race I wouldn't be saying that at all. We did just beat Two of Diamonds, trained by Barry Hills, by a neck. But the ground wasn't great ground, and Willie Carson went to the stand rails. He ended up tracking back to the far side. Troy had travelled a good bit further than the field.

'Both colts worked round Major Hern's special Derby gallop at West Ilsley, before Epsom. Troy coasted round. No problem at all with the undulations, or turning left-handed and the downhill finish. You can always teach them, but some take a lot longer to learn than others. They learn through repetition, like kids. With Henbit, it was just natural. By then, two weeks before Epsom, we knew for sure that he was good. His coat shone and he'd matured and strengthened at the right time. For us, the only doubt about the race after that was that the owner, Mme Plesch, wanted to run him in the French Derby. We could see why. After all, Mme Plesch lived in France. It meant we all had to hang back from having a bet on him. When we wanted to, he was 50–1. But then he wasn't sure to run. In the end we had to make do with 20–1. I don't think Mme Plesch ever actually came to the yard. The perfect owner, Bill Wightman would say – lives abroad and corresponds by cheque.'

McCann rates Troy just ahead of Henbit. The latter was sadly missed on the gallops after his Derby injury. 'He was a good horse, for sure,' McCann says. 'Not quite up there with Troy – or the likes of Nashwan, for that matter, still to come – but good, tough and honest. For those weeks leading up to the Derby, Henbit shone like a beacon. I always think back

to a day on the gallops with him as a two-year-old. The
Major told me to lead off and then quicken up at the two
marker to give the others something to aim at. I did what I
was told and waited, and waited. There was no sign of the
pack. I peeked back, and those behind me were all
absolutely flat to the boards, while I was still cruising.
Afterwards, the Major collared me. "You went too fast,
Mac!" "But I was only in second gear," I said. "If you were
in second gear then he is a f***ing champion," said the
Major. He could swear all right with the best and the rest of
us. He whipped away on his hack in disbelief.

'The worst thing about losing a good horse like Henbit
is that he can't bring the others on. You gallop them with the
rest of the string and some horses are beaten six lengths,
then two weeks later you notice that some of the pack are
being beaten only three lengths. They are getting better. Like
kids, again, they want to keep up and are brought on.'

*

Dayjur was an altogether more straightforward proposition
– pure speed. At least after some early faltering steps. 'At
two, we took him round the indoor ride, where the sand is
pretty deep,' McCann recalls. 'A bit of metal had fallen off
the tractor and was buried. Dayjur trod on it. His career
nearly ended there and then before he'd even run. He was
cut, quite severely. But the metal just missed his tendon. It
set him back maybe three weeks. We were very, very lucky.
That could have been it.

'I rode him at two and three. When you were in the saddle, you'd feel him change his legs about twenty times in a canter. It wasn't that he was tearing away with you; he'd just be idle in front, waiting for the real job. Then you'd give him a little squeeze and that was it. He just left them. He wasn't the best mover, and he wasn't particularly tall either. Not a bull of a horse, and nothing special when he worked as a two-year-old. I'd ride him along with the Major's mile-and-a-quarter types and he was quite ordinary. He didn't pull much. He wasn't a typically hyped-up sprinter.'

Those early efforts required a reassessment. 'You might remember that he ran over seven furlongs. The Major always wanted them to stay a mile, for the Guineas. You could tell him and tell him that this doesn't get a mile, or even seven, but he'd still have a go. With Dayjur, he had to concede from the work he was doing and from the results at the track. He was beaten at Newbury, held up. There was no denying it – a sprinter. After that was resolved, the work was simple. We'd pull him out and just let him go. He'd be fifteen lengths clear every time, even over as little as four furlongs, which was his usual work trip. Nothing could stay with him. He'd give other horses head starts. It didn't matter; he'd be gone. Everything changed when we realised he was a five-furlong horse.'

Only Dayjur's propensity to jump confounded. 'When Dayjur won the 1990 Prix de l'Abbaye before going to America,' McCann observes, 'you'll see him have a look at the hoardings. He was easily in front and entering idle mode, and that was when he would shy from things. When the job was done, his mind would wander. I was actually in Tenerife when he ran in the Breeders' Cup. It was all so quick. I couldn't really take in what had happened. In all my time in racing I have never known anything like it. He stayed in America so we never saw him again. No chance to explain himself!

'Before the Breeders' Cup, we had an American lad working with us at the time. When Dayjur started to burn off the competition, the Major asked him how our boy would compare with the Americans straight out of the stalls. He said, "He'd still be in them when the rest would be on their way, as they start with a bell not the gates." A couple of days later the Major was out on the gallops with a pair of handbells, training Dayjur to kick-start just like in the Seabiscuit film. If you look at the Breeders' Cup Sprint where he was drawn wide, you'll see that he was in front after a furlong. He made virtually all the running that day.

'He didn't have off days. Dayjur was very professional. He always delivered on the gallops. Confident, straightforward, no attitude, uncomplicated.'

Nashwan might not have had the raw, instant pace of Dayjur, but McCann insists he also had plenty of speed. 'Nashwan wouldn't have beaten Dayjur in a sprint, but he would have been too good for most. If you stop the tape of him in the Guineas in May 1989 after six furlongs, they are flat to the boards, including Danehill, who went on to be a champion sprinter. Nashwan's still cruising. His perfect trip was probably a mile and a quarter. At Epsom, over twelve furlongs, it helped that the finish is downhill. He was just so superior. He had the speed to lob along, then you would ask him to race for just the six furlongs, so stamina never really came into it.'

Nashwan's full range became apparent in good time. 'He was like a boxer or athlete: he had controlled aggression. Underneath his skin he was quite competitive, but he channelled it beautifully. He never showed a temper. A beautiful mover, too. We knew about Unfuwain, his half-brother, and Height of Fashion, their dam. We realised when we started working him at the back end of his two-year-old season that he was really special, even better than the pair of them. Before that point, Nashwan wouldn't have been as good as, say, Alhaarth – a speed horse – at two. At two he had just the two races, at Newbury and Ascot. He was even money for his first race, at Newbury, and we all knew that he would win. In fact, the second horse came across the course so he travelled further. We won only narrowly so you'd think, "Might have beaten us." But he never would. When he came back to the yard he looked more like a racehorse, and his work from that point on just got better and better. Still, races like the Dewhurst simply weren't an option. Physically, he wasn't even on schedule for the Guineas the following spring. He was a big horse, a late developer.

'Unfuwain had impressed the season before, and at three. Height of Fashion was quite similar to Nashwan.

Perhaps she showed more at two. He was always maturing at two. She was probably more forward. Unfuwain was even more like Height of Fashion than Nashwan. Like her, he was more spirited. When I rode her over the winter of 1981/82 between her two-year-old and Classic season there was plenty of snow. We'd sweep out a strip for her to work on. She'd stop and wouldn't go on. She was still doing the same in June at that very spot. Lots of spirit and character. Unfuwain was the same – a big bull of a horse, a schoolyard bully with a temper he wasn't slow to show. He'd stand there looking at you. Very boisterous as a young horse, always happy and messing about. The more he worked, the more he settled down. The Major changed his box once to try and calm him down, but he had to change it back. Unfuwain simply couldn't cope with a sudden switch like that. The same with Nayef, who won the Champion, International and Prince of Wales's Stakes in 2001, 2002 and 2003 respectively. He was a little bit edgy as a two-year-old, but the more he did, the better he became. The whole family was like that. Nashwan was just that bit more professional about things, and better.'

A change of plan required the Major to up the tempo. 'Nashwan wasn't ever on schedule for the 2,000 Guineas over the winter of 1988/89. His owner, Hamdan Al-Maktoum, had Al Hareb for the race. He was more suitably bred for the Guineas and had won the 1988 Racing Post Trophy the season before. He was right on schedule. Nashwan also threw a splint after Christmas, so we had to stop with him. He was just walking round a sand circuit in January 1989. We called it the sin bin. For the first official work morning in March, he was still in there. But as the spring progressed it became clear that Al Hareb just wasn't going to be good enough for the Guineas. He just didn't come on. The Major decided to give Nashwan a run. That was it. Suddenly, we had to give Nashwan a rushed prep for the Guineas. Instead of one prep race then the Derby, which was the original plan, it was a race at the end of April. The splint settled down – just about. The problem was how to get enough work into him. As we stepped things up, he became quite unbalanced. Feed was also important. Luckily, he was always a very good eater. He needed to strengthen quickly.' Fortunately, as McCann said, Nashwan did exactly that.

'We had a stretch of gallop, about a mile and a quarter,' McCann continues. 'It was like the very best carpet – beautiful turf. We all called the stretch "the trial gallop". We'd use it only three or four times a year. It was close to the Guineas, and the Major told me to lead off. We had no sticks. The first one who passed me would be the winner. Nashwan and I went fifteen lengths clear even without a whip. The Major said, "The Brigadier [Gerard, who won the 2,000 Guineas in 1971] wouldn't have done that." At 8.30 in the morning he was 33-1 for Newmarket; by midday he was down to 8–1; and by mid-afternoon he was the 3–1 favourite.

'After the Guineas we left him alone a bit. The Derby

was academic. He was spot on that day. At West Ilsley when we won a Classic there was always a party at the village hall. With Nashwan, the hall was booked a week before the Guineas. So was the disco. We knew. Then, after the Guineas, we booked the hall again straight away for after the Derby. It wasn't like booking a room in Newmarket. Everyone would know then. West Ilsley was more of a farming community. The yard was part of everyone's life. Our horses were their horses.

'After the Derby the Major gave Nashwan every chance for the rest of the 1989 season, right up to his last run, in the Prix Niel. For that he arranged for him to go to Stansted airport in a horsebox for a trial run before the race, which was his prep for the Arc. It meant that when it was for real Nashwan wouldn't be spooked at all by the road trip. The thing was that we all knew Nashwan was finished after the Eclipse and King George. He grew a little bit during the summer. He was still a bit weak. Those two races against the older horses, that was the end of him. His work wasn't ever as good as it had been. You don't have easy races at his level, and his preparation for the Guineas had been rushed. The Eclipse meant he had to take on older horses in early July. To my mind, he was given a lot to do on dead ground. They went nearly ten lengths clear of him so he had to pick up Opening Verse – Indian Skimmer's lead horse and a pretty good one in his own right – and was then ridden all the way to the line to win. He had also got a bit worked up in the days leading up to the Eclipse. After the Eclipse, the first time he cantered, things were different. The Major asked me how he was. I told him I thought he was knackered. He couldn't care if he walked, cantered or galloped. He was just very tired. For the King George, he needed a lead horse. Not to make the pace, but actually to hold them up. Look at the tapes of the race – Nashwan's pulling. At the time, the Major was quite surprised. "It took them a while to work out that the pacemaker was in there to slow the field down," he said. Greville Starkey, who rode Cacoethes, realised too late. At least not too late for us.'

In the end, it was just the unique sequence of Guineas, Derby, Eclipse and King George. 'The thing about Nashwan was that he had a really competitive spirit,' McCann says. 'He loved passing horses. He'd be on the gallops and you would just have to edge him out. He was gone.'

*

At Kingwood, there is a corner that is West Ilsley, a plate of the Oaks and St Leger winner Dunfermline taking pride of place on the front door of McCann's home. The Queen, like all Hern's owners, benefited from her trainer's attention to detail. 'You can imagine that Dunfermline's two Classics for the Queen were fantastic,' McCann enthuses. 'For the yard, they really set us apart. We'd also had Highclere's 1,000 Guineas in 1974 for the Queen. Very flighty, very hyper filly, always fresh.

'When the Major retired, he laid out all the plates he'd kept and gave us the pick. I still joke today that this was how I ended up with plates from Nashwan's Derby. Sold a good two dozen of those since! I actually picked a plate that Dunfermline really did wear. I rode her through the summer of her Classic wins, on and off. She was, I think, the only filly to beat Alleged, which she managed in the St Leger. Plus she won the Oaks, all for the Queen in Jubilee year! Everyone who was at West Ilsley in 1977 remembers that. We didn't win the Derby, but that wasn't for a lack of trying. We ran three in the race, but no luck. The Oaks in those days was on Saturday, after the Derby on Wednesday. We had the disappointment, then the fairytale. Dunfermline had a little break after the Oaks. You can't make them much fitter at that stage in the season; it's all about keeping them sweet. She came back into work for the St Leger and went a mile and a half before the race. Another Classic extended the Jubilee parties.'

In those days, there was only the one detective for Her Majesty. 'We'd always look forward to her coming to the yard,' McCann recalls. 'And we always knew she was on her way. It was simple: just look out for the Land Rover being cleaned in the morning. Later in the day the Major would have us in to say she was due the next day. We already knew.' Sometimes she'd come at the weekend. 'She came one Saturday morning when we were suffering from a virus. We had just enough healthy ones for first lot, but for second lot we in truth had only about nine to gallop. The Queen would usually come for first lot – you'd soon become accustomed to her being around in just a headscarf and a pair of wellingtons – then breakfast with the Major and go off again. We thought, "Everything will be fine." As you'd have it, this time she was delayed and arrived for second lot. That meant just nine to gallop with another twenty or so limited to the indoor gallop.

'From that point on, things just got worse. Once the Queen had arrived, I led off on a colt. Shortly after kicking off I was passed by a filly, without rider or saddle and flying. Needless to say, she was owned by the Queen. The Queen was with the then Lord Porchester [her racing manager; later Lord Carnarvon]. At the top of the gallop she watched as her horse, having dumped her rider, continued to run loose while the rest of us cringed. All we could do was wait. Of course, she eventually rejoined the string. The Major said we should just walk her back. The Queen and Lord Porchester drove back in the Land Rover. At the bottom of the gallop they got out to stop the traffic, Porchester on one side of the road, the Queen on the other side. When we got back to the yard we formed a human chain to usher the filly into a box. The Queen was part of the chain.'

Lady Beaverbrook was an occasional visitor to the yard. More often, certainly, than Dick Hollingsworth, and more welcome than some others. 'We had a phone call one day from Number Ten Downing Street. A dignitary was due to make a state visit. Could he be shown the gallops? The Major exploded. "I haven't time for that!" he shouted. "I have horses to train!" Then another call came in from what you might say was a slightly higher office. So, thanks to the Palace, the dignitary came in the end. The detectives actually arrived the night before, and there were sniffer dogs on the day. This fellow arrived with outriders in a car with a flag on the front. Compare that to the minimal fuss when the Queen visited. Then, when he got out of the car, we all realised he wasn't even Willie Carson's height.

'Lady Beaverbrook, who owned the likes of Bustino, would come to the yard when she could, but she was only allowed into the country for 90 days or so because of the taxman. She chose carefully and made sure she had days in reserve for the racecourse. At any one time she would have about twenty horses with us. I usually looked after two for her. She'd sometimes give me, and other grooms who looked after her string, a thank you. One day she started off by handing out £50 a horse. After the first ten she was running out of cash, so it went down to just £20 a horse. The lads who went short moaned like hell, as anyone would. The Major made up the difference, which in the case of the lad who looked after Bustino was deserved. At first, he could be a tricky one. But he was always a good-looking horse. He'd be black with sweat on the gallops. The more he did, the more he settled down. He was always a good worker, always easy without being super or brilliant. We expected Bustino to beat Grundy in the 1975 King George. At the time in the yard, we were all part of a syndicate which shared in a cut of the prize money the stable won. Instead of dishing out everyone's share that was due, we had the lot on Bustino to win. We needed Lady Beaverbrook's generosity after that.

'Dick Hollingsworth was one owner we never saw at the yard. I think he was a real recluse. His horses were always a bit wayward. You'd certainly look out for them. And at first he'd never let us run them as two-year-olds. Then the Major persuaded him otherwise and in no time won him the Champagne Stakes at Goodwood. Kept him happy enough. Still no visit, mind.'

*

McCann splits his time with the Major in two: before 1984 and his hunting accident, which left him in a wheelchair, and after that year, a period that includes the time when the lease to West Ilsley was not renewed. 'The best of the Major was on the gallops,' McCann says. 'Before his accident, he loved the riding. He'd be upsides you, tell you a joke, and then he would ask you to tell him one. He loved to laugh. He'd join us for third lot during the winter. We'd be freezing, riding out the part of the string that wasn't in the best of health, the misbehaviours, and he'd still join us. Good fun. Very hard but very fair.

'The business of the lease was very stressful for everyone. With the horses in the morning, we just got on with things. The job itself was a release. We had less time to worry. What you must remember about West Ilsley is that the yard's more like a village. There were about 26 houses and the Major's staff lived there. The boss gets the sack? Think about it. There was a really dark period when we didn't know at all what was happening. Pressmen were hiding in trees and bushes. The Major called me in and said if there were reporters hanging around he'd rather they spoke to me than everyone else, one by one. Public relations might not have been the Major's strongest point, but he showed he did understand how these things work, even back then. It was the same with the Stable Lads' Association. When we started up, he called me in. "I'd rather that you were involved in it, so put yourself forward," he said.

'The Major was tough on the horses, but in a kind way. He kept them fresh enough and would never overdo it with big races ahead. On the gallops, counting down the days to the Guineas or the Derby, the lead horse wouldn't be of the calibre to stretch the Classic horses before the time was right. We'd have a slow horse in front to slow everyone down. He always trod a very fine line. The good horses would not often take each other on, until the time was right, and then probably only once. He also had a tendency to keep the same rider on the potentially good ones. That way you'd have a better chance of knowing straight away if there was something untoward. If you changed riders every week, how could they know for sure when things were wrong? He always took every precaution. For Epsom, he'd always send two horseboxes: one with the runner, and another one following behind just in case the first one broke down. Of course, it never did. But it might have done.

'He was always very focused on getting the very best out of the horses. He'd let them come to hand in their own time. With the two-year-olds, they started galloping at the end of April. The Major really wouldn't ever rush them, no matter how good they were. I remember one year on the first official work day for two-year-olds, I was riding this big, tall horse. The Major asked me what I thought. "Good, but not spectacular," I said. The result of that comment was that the Major put him away for six weeks, with future races already in mind. With York coming up, the Major stepped him up. He raced there, and won easily, beating a Group winner. The horse was called Gorytus.'

Plenty, however, posed the Major problems. 'Ela-Mana-Mou arrived at West Ilsley as a four-year-old, when Lord Weinstock bought him. He wouldn't eat at first. They all do in the end as they get hungry eventually, but if there is a race ahead you have to get the food into them. He was never very robust, and this didn't help. Of course, he won the King George VI and Queen Elizabeth Stakes for us in 1980. But I think his frame meant that he just wasn't strong enough to win races like, say, the Prix de l'Arc de Triomphe. That can be a slog – not for him. He'd be more like racing's version of Sebastian Coe.

'Sea Anchor was one of Mr Hollingsworth's stayers. A really strong horse. He once started fighting with his galloping partner. Bireme was another Hollingsworth homebred who won the Oaks, in 1980. She was also a handful. A good two-year-old, but when we started preparing her for Epsom she didn't show us much at all. We sent her up the gallops, and she finished last. Then we tried a few different approaches – last again. Trials like the Musidora were coming up. So the Major told me to take her out on her own, on a Thursday, which was a non-work day for the rest of the yard. We also put a pair of blinkers on her. We jumped off at the bottom of the hill and let her go as fast as she could manage. I really worked her hard. She didn't quite make it to the top of the hill, but by the end of the work she was completely knackered. She was a filly who might just have known a bit too much about the game, and this was the Major's way of kidding her into some proper work. With her it was the last resort, but it worked.

'In my early days, the yearlings that came in would be much more of a handful. We'd call them "long tails". They would have been left out in fields and their tails would have grown down to the ground. Only then would we receive the raw material. The Major was like a sculptor, turning these big blocks of stone into art.'

With Sun Princess, the Major's patience paid off. 'Sun Princess took time,' McCann recalls. 'If she had been able to settle she'd have been even better than she was. She never did. She was so genuine. As a two-year-old, she showed us everything. At two, the Major ran her over six furlongs in the Blue Seal at Ascot because he knew there would be plenty of pace. Over a mile it would have been a bad experience for her. The only problem was getting her down to the start. She finished second that day – not bad for a twelve-furlong horse racing over six. Classic horses have to have the speed.

'At three, in 1983, she produced the best gallop I've ever seen, before she ran in the Oaks. It was a full mile-and-a-half stretch with the second half downhill like at Epsom. I led off on Little Wolf with Sun Princess behind us. I had backed her at 40–1 for the Oaks and I remember thinking, "I've done my money here." What had happened was at the top of the hill, when I was two lengths in front, Sun Princess took a pull just as I kicked. So at that point I was actually ten lengths ahead of her. Then she got going again. She simply made up the ground and went straight past us. Right from her days as a two-year-old, she always pulled. We tried everything. We cantered her with the hack, we tried to give her plenty of rein, to take hold of her, to go dead slow, just trot and sit in behind other horses. Nothing worked. You might say that she ran away with Willie Carson in the Oaks. That was just her. It is not something that training nurtures in them. It is just that they want to work in fifth gear rather than second. She'd have been like that if she had stayed in training until she was eight. Relkino was another.

'The secret to riding horses like that is how you set off,' McCann explains. 'Once you have lost them, once you had lost Sun Princess, she was gone. You have to start with a roll, then be strong and brave. What you really want to do is to set them up on a loose rein. But that is always a risk, as once they are gone, they are gone. Then again, some pull at home but not at the racecourse, and some are the opposite. A mystery.' Today, McCann can still recall the Major's wise words. 'Watching on the gallops, he would always say,

"Better lazy than one who pulls." You'd say, "He's an idle so-and-so," and the Major would reply, "Don't worry about that. They are easier to start than stop."'

CHAPTER SEVEN

STUART MESSENGER AND JIMMY SCOTT

*From Shergar, golden years
with Sir Michael Stoute*

As brothers-in-law, Stuart Messenger and Jimmy Scott have long been related. But in their case the bond has an added dimension. Professionally speaking, they are also family. Between them they can boast over 60 years working for Sir Michael Stoute at his Freemason Lodge stables in Newmarket. Home for them is up the Bury Road, after you have left the town's high street. Messenger's flat actually overlooks the first colts' yard.

There is a pleasing simplicity to Messenger's CV – just the single name of Stoute (he had avoided employment as a carpet salesman: his mother arranged the interview, he never showed). Scott's career has seen him climb the ladder to the very top, a period that included a spell with Cecil Boyd-Rochfort. Scott pre-dates the trainer's knighthood by many years, having been at the yard since day one, in 1972, when Stoute first took out a licence to train in his own name.

The all-stars that have passed through Stoute's hands since then are testimony to the wise choice the pair made to stick around. Shergar alone would be reason to look back with a sense of satisfaction. Messenger jokes that everyone who has worked for Stoute claims to have ridden the tragically kidnapped Shergar, but he and Jimmy really did. To the roll of honour can be added names like Shahrastani and Kris Kin – both, like Shergar, winners of the Epsom Derby – and fillies such as Sonic Lady, Pure Grain and Aliysa. The last-named was robbed, Messenger and Scott agree, of her Oaks after a positive post-race drugs test that still baffles them. There are other Classic winners such as King's Best, speed machines such as Ajdal (after a flirtation with middle distances), and Zilzal, who like King's Best was a case of patience rewarded amid all the sweat. Incidentally, Scott rates Shahrastani's Irish Derby win as superior to Shergar's success in the same race.

In case you think that there is anything conservative in Messenger and Scott for staying with the same employer for such a stretch, consider for a moment the stamps in their passports as a result. Accompanying Pilsudski and Singspiel in their bids to make up for missing out on Classic success – the two names sit well together after many a shared excursion – Messenger and Scott have seen the world. As well as regular trips to Ireland – including the year when Sonic Lady's passport was left at the yard – and mainland Europe, the duo have been west for the Breeders' Cup and the best of American racing's prizes, and also east to Hong Kong, Japan and Australia. Messenger was on hand in America to bring back Singspiel, a wounded warrior, across the Atlantic.

Whatever air miles Messenger and Scott have clocked up, the focus of their endeavour is the goings-on at home, at Freemason Lodge. Also in residence remains Kribensis, shaped towards successes at the Cheltenham Festival by Scott's hands and now, as the stable's hack, just about mellowed with age. Scott's gifts as a work rider remain key to the team, as well as his skills in accompanying the string's best on the road as Stoute's travelling head lad. Based at the yard, Messenger, now Stoute's head man and no slouch in the saddle himself in days gone by, applies the methods he learnt from the late Andy Andrews. He never rushed to the vet's cabinet when nature might have a remedy, so neither does his apprentice. Every day poses a new challenge probably solvable with an old solution.

In the morning, when the colts start baying for their feed, it is Messenger who hears the dawn call from his flat and obliges at what for him is the best part of the day. 'Looking out on the yard in the morning sunshine, before the staff arrive, hearing the horses shout for their feed – heaven,' he says. As a Yorkshireman in exile, he has found a southern haven for God's own people. 'Riding a proper racehorse is awesome,' he reflects. His mind drifts back to days in the saddle up the gallops when a career over jumps was briefly entertained as alternative employment. 'The ground they cover, the stride, the power,' he whispers, in awe. Scott adds that his own time there bears full testimony to Messenger's experiences.

*

Messenger had only recently arrived in the yard from Yorkshire when Shergar was resident. Scott already had nearly a decade with Stoute against his name – two when Shahrastani pulled in. 'I was still finding my feet when Shergar won the Derby in 1981,' Messenger recalls. 'I had been with Sir Michael – though he wasn't Sir Michael yet – for just the two years. You listened to the more experienced lads to find out which of the two-year-olds were rated. He did stand out all right, you could see that. He looked the part, and was a bit flashy with a white blaze and wild eye.' Later, Scott would partner Shahrastani. 'Compared to Shergar? Chalk and cheese on the gallops,' Scott says with a laugh. 'Shahrastani was so laid back, while Shergar was always very strong, even to lead up at the races. He was a very proud walker. We knew that Shergar was good all right as pretty soon we started having problems laying up with him. If you were riding him you wouldn't realise that you were going well. Then you'd look round and the rest were miles behind you. On Shergar you just didn't feel like you were travelling it was so smooth – but you were, for sure. He was a kind horse too, and very professional about business at the races. He did very well over the winter from two to three. You notice that if you go on holiday. You come back and think, "Yes, that's progress." As a three-year-old he would be the strongest I have ever ridden. You always had to have your wits around you when you had something that powerful underneath.

'He got loose just before the Derby,' Messenger recalls. 'I remember being told that they had finally caught up with him at Henry Cecil's yard. It was all over before I really knew what was happening. I learnt that he had got loose, galloped off, and was then told he was now safe. You look back now and think, "Jeepers, the Derby favourite loose and galloping down Moulton Road?"'

'Word spread,' remembers Scott. 'Was he safe? What happened? The story went right round town. Favourite for the Derby, loose in the town.'

'Maybe it was the extra bit of work he needed,' jokes Messenger.

'If we have a runner in the Derby they sometimes go the opposite way round a gallop to get a feel for turning left-handed,' Scott confides. 'Or, on occasion, we have put a rail up near Lord Derby's stud to try and recreate a little bit of the camber and turn of Epsom. Gallops like that just give horses a feel for what is coming. But Shergar was so well balanced, naturally, plus he had been round Chester. If you can go round there as well as he did, you can go anywhere after that.'

'I remember Shergar also went over to racecourse side in Newmarket,' adds Messenger. 'I think the idea was that if they go the wrong way round there it is as if there is a little dip on the way down with some camber, and also a dip on the turn too, so it helps prepare them for Epsom.'

'One morning we galloped down the Limekilns,' says Scott. 'A fellow called Dicky, who would ride Shergar most often on the gallops, said that he didn't think he was sound. The boss asked me to get on him. I just cantered him very gently down the middle of the gallop. He was fine. I don't think I have ever been so pleased after a gallop as on that day.'

After the Derby, Messenger enjoyed the relief of success. 'I remember that the yard was absolutely buzzing. After Epsom we decorated the stable van with a big banner and drove it through town. It made you proud to be part of the team. Then in the mornings after Epsom, Shergar would be up front of everyone taking us to the gallops, like he was our leader.'

'He seemed to know after Epsom that he had done something really special,' reckons Scott.

Shahrastani, carrying the same silks in 1986, had much to live up to. 'I rode Shahrastani a lot as a two-year-old,' Scott recalls. 'There was another colt that everyone in the yard was very sweet on and plenty fancied for the Derby, but he never did anything. I can't even remember his name now. I'd rate Shahrastani as the best staying horse I have ever ridden. On the gallops he was absolutely straightforward, like a pet. When he was fresh he could rear up on you, but apart from that he was so friendly. He loved to be made a fuss of. I suppose in that way he was slightly feminine, almost like a filly. We'd go into his horsebox at night and give him a sod of grass. He'd love that. He knew you and would begin to look for it. At the races he could become a little nervous on his way to the start, so I would always lead him, but it was just that he wanted company. He loved having you around. He was very kind all the time he was with us.

'People underrated Shahrastani. The reason for this was that he didn't show you a lot at home. He fooled plenty. It wasn't that he was lazy, just that everything he did do you had to ask him to do. Otherwise you would think that he was just an ordinary horse. In the saddle, you might fall asleep on him. But once you had asked him to show you what he had, you knew he had the gears all right. You only had to give him a squeeze and he would quicken. A beautiful ride. In the yard we actually thought he was as good as Shergar. He certainly won the Irish Derby more convincingly. He had been very weak as a two-year-old but grew and strengthened. To my mind he would have been a cracking four-year-old. Remember that pretty much everything that stayed in training for a season, having been beaten by him, won at four.

'I was very confident about Epsom after he won the Sandown Classic Trial and I backed him then at 16–1. That race was much more important then than it is today. I remember Willie Carson coming up to me afterwards and saying, "He'll never win a Derby." I never paid any attention to that. With Epsom in mind, he didn't have the best of knees. They were very open, which is terrible for coming down hills. Yet he still came round Tattenham Corner at Epsom when really good movers wouldn't thrive on the slope and camber there.

'Travelling-wise, he only once had a terrible journey on a plane, going to Ireland for the Irish Derby at the Curragh. It was a really rough passage on a seriously windy day and the flight was pretty rough. On the plane he took the skin off his head. There was never a problem with flying after that, like on the plane to Paris for the Prix de l'Arc de Triomphe. The experience never seemed to affect him. Wherever they were, he was never a problem after any of his races. Even after the Derby, which was a hard race for him, he kept his condition. He was, as we say, a good doer, and he liked his feed.'

Scott literally treasures his memory. 'I have a lovely bronze of him that the Aga Khan gave me at the end of the season,' he says. 'It is still on my table today. In my view, Shahrastani was undervalued. He was such a competitive horse on the racecourse, and he never really got the recognition he deserved for beating Dancing Brave in the Derby. That day, Dancing Brave simply didn't come down the hill at Epsom.'

'Shahrastani showed me that you don't need to be brilliant on the gallops at home to be great on the course,' Messenger adds. 'I learnt not to judge them too quickly. I also began to get the hang of the routine for winning the Derby. Shergar, Shahrastani – I know, now, that we always have a party. I remember thinking it was brilliant. Also something like the bronze Jimmy received from the Aga Khan. That's more special than any amount of money.'

*

Pure Grain tested the lateral thinking of Scott. He and Messenger had to use all their ingenuity to keep fillies such as her, Sonic Lady, Milligram and Colorspin sweet. 'Pure Grain won the Irish and Yorkshire Oaks in 1995 – strange,' Scott recalls. 'She hated going into a box on her own. At the yard, that was fine. Wherever she was stabled was separated by bars so she could always see her neighbour. But when she was travelling in a horsebox she'd get lonely. We had to take a mirror with us. With that she was more than happy. She'd think there was another horse travelling too.'

Colorspin's slimline frame has stuck in Messenger's mind. 'She was like a greyhound, with nothing on her,' he says. 'Her backside was like a cow, with her hips sticking out. Apart from her head, she was really nothing special. She was only an average feeder and she wouldn't take more feed on than she'd want. If the RSPCA had seen her in the paddock they would have taken her away. There was really nothing to her at all. But she could certainly run.'

'Like Fair Salinia,' Scott suggests. 'She won the Oaks in 1978, our first Classic winner, but we had to nail the saddle on her. They can sometimes look like that, especially the fillies. But she could run all right. I remember Colorspin's head – really bonny. I liked Milligram too.' But Sonic Lady was the pick. 'I rode her as a yearling,' says Scott. 'I said to the girl who looked after her – Elaine, who was tragically killed in a car crash – "This is a machine." Sonic Lady absolutely stood out. She was outstanding. She gave you this feel. It is very hard to explain. I guess it must be the feel you get when you drive a Rolls-Royce. Even at that very young age, as a yearling, you feel it. I didn't ride her after that but I could see that she was getting stronger and stronger. She was built more like a colt, which can often be the case with good fillies. Very powerful shoulders. She was also a pretty complex character. We had to work to keep her settled and cool. As a three-year-old she had a special bit which really helped. I think it came from France. If I remember rightly, I think it was Elaine's idea. We always had to be careful with Sonic Lady as she could become quite strung out. In general, her temperament was really good, but it is true that she could get a bit buzzy. That wasn't from the extra feed or work when a big race was near, but just because of the way she was. There were times when she was no trouble at all. Travelling, she was fine. You just had to be careful where you took her. The Al Bahathri gallop would have been perfect for her and she always wanted to work up gallops that were familiar and which she liked, but that stretch hadn't been built in 1985 when she came into training.

'Colorspin was less versatile; she always needed her ground. But she was a very good traveller. Milligram was another one from Meon Valley Stud. You could always pick out the families. I rode her a couple of times. All the ones we had from Meon Valley seemed to be good. They all had really great temperaments.'

Aliysa still stirs a mix of emotions. 'She had the heart of a lion,' says Scott. 'You always knew with her that she would give you 100 per cent. She wasn't anything to look at, really, and was so laid back. Girls could ride her, no problem, and you wouldn't notice that she'd even worked. After she won her maiden at Wolverhampton she just improved and improved. She was very athletic. On the gallops, she could really lengthen and was very balanced. At home, you can pick the ones who will struggle at Epsom, as they haven't got that.'

'With the positive test after the 1989 Oaks I just thought that they had made a mistake,' Messenger says. 'A mystery to everyone at the yard. We had always been very strict on the medical records. To us, she's still an Oaks winner. It was gutting because we really didn't know why she had lost the race. It was also a great pity that she didn't win at the Curragh in the Irish Oaks, like Sonic Lady did in the Guineas. Mind you, we forgot her passport when she travelled to Ireland. There was a right panic here. Fax machines had just about come out. We had to go to the post office to send a copy of the document through. First time they'd accepted anything other than the real document. Bit of luck, that.'

*

By the time Kris Kin won the Derby in 2003, Messenger was head lad and fed the colts. With this one, as well as food,

Messenger had to provide a massage service. 'He loved his food. His first run wasn't great but he was a typical improving Stoute horse. We probably thought, "This is a nice handicapper who could win a decent race," but our expectations weren't much more than that. He just seemed lazy. As a yearling he was easy enough to break in, and as a two-year-old he was just in with the others. For most of his career he was ridden by girls. He just got to know their voices. He was certainly nothing to write home about or make you chase ante-post bets. I thought he had a nice rich colour, but even after the winter he was no more than ordinary to my mind. If I am honest about it, not one of my real favourites at the time. Chester, where he won the Dee Stakes, at least showed us that he was serious. We thought, "Well, we haven't got anything else to go to the Derby with so he is our Derby horse almost by default."'

'Kris Kin certainly had the right temperament,' Scott suggests. 'That has been true of all the Derby winners we have had at the yard. It makes a hell of a difference to them being able to produce on the day. But I rode him one day and remember coming back to the office and saying that I thought he might make up into a Group horse, maybe somewhere like Italy.'

If Messenger hadn't got up before dawn on Derby day, Kris Kin might not have exceeded Scott's expectations. 'On the Thursday night, with the Derby on Saturday, Kris Kin was as stiff as anything,' Messenger remembers. 'We thought, "This isn't going to gallop up Newmarket's straight mile let alone down Epsom with a camber and slope." Watching him walk, we thought, "That's it." Things weren't much better on the Friday.

'For the Derby, we'd usually travel down the night before. The boss said that we were better off leaving him here for some physio, rather than travelling. At least in the yard we could try and treat the stiffness. So we got our machines on him. I got up at three a.m. on Derby morning, fed Kris Kin, then put him on the horse walker for an hour. Next we put on the physio massage machines to try and loosen him up. When we had finished he'd certainly improved on the night before, but you are talking Epsom, and we have had some sound horses come back from there in a terrible state.

'Looking back at the way he was, it wouldn't have surprised me if he had some trouble of sorts that we couldn't work out. He was never ridden over a full twelve furlongs before the Derby, and I don't remember him being taken anywhere like racecourse side for a pre-Derby gallop like past runners. The most he did was on the Al Bahathri gallop, which is a mile that runs down a bit then climbs up very slightly, and he'd have had a canter the opposite way round the gallop just to help him learn to turn. No reason to think, "Ah, that's why he's so stiff." Kevin Bradshaw, who rode him a lot, would never hassle him and left him to get on with it. I remember that whenever Kevin thought the horse was in great form he gave him just a gentle blow-out. That was all he needed to keep him at his peak. Maybe it was the pressure in preparing for the Derby. They do have to be spot on. With hindsight, it was probably lucky that Kevin didn't get into him more on the gallops in those final pieces of work. Just imagine – he would have been even stiffer.'

'On the gallops he didn't show you anything at all,' Scott adds. 'He would always finish a neck up. Not like Shergar, who would go at least ten lengths clear. Looking back, it was as if he knew that he had done what was required of him and would then pull up. Even in his final piece of work before the Derby he'd have been half a furlong behind his lead horse. He was so laid back in the mornings, you were always guessing with him.'

No doubts after the Derby, though. 'When he came back from Epsom, we had decorated his box,' Messenger remembers. 'After all the work, it was quite emotional to win. Funnily enough, after the race he wasn't really stiff at all. Certainly no worse a state than you would expect any horse to be in after running in a Classic. And he was never worse than he was on the day before the Derby. After that we kept the massage machines going before a race, but stiffness was never a serious problem again.'

*

Pilsudski and Singspiel, of course, took Messenger and Scott further afield than Epsom for their greatest success. 'I shipped them to Canada for the Breeders' Cup in 1996,' Scott recalls. 'I rode Pilsudski, Kevin Bradshaw rode Singspiel, and all the talk was about Singspiel. But we both said to the boss, "If anything does manage to beat him it will be our other one." And Pilsudski did win in the end, with Singspiel second.'

'I was with Singspiel for the Japan Cup in 1996,' says Messenger. 'Before the race, Kevin rode Singspiel again in his final piece of work at the Tokyo track, and we stood on the bend. Even from behind the rails you could see the power under him. Me and all the lads just looked at each other and ran down to see him at the end of the gallop. John McCririck, the Channel 4 broadcaster, who was also there, saw us and said, "You look happy."'

Opera House was a good yardstick for the older horses. 'He won the King George in 1993 and had a beautiful head,' says Scott. 'Opera House actually looked like a filly. Singspiel was the same alongside Pilsudski. Opera House never put much condition on but he always looked healthy. His coat always stood out, from early spring. He was very exuberant when he was well. He'd swing a leg out just because he was feeling so good and confident. He'd just be saying to you, "When do we go? I'm ready." With Singspiel, it was progress between three and four that made him. Even then he still wasn't that robust compared to Pilsudski. He was this huge, big colt – big everywhere. Even at five, Singspiel still kept something of his feminine looks. Well beaten at two by Celtic Swing at Ascot. I think after that some thought that he wasn't going to be that special.'

'With Singspiel, it was a case of having to fiddle the feed into him,' Messenger remembers. 'Some are like that. You have to think about the horse and how to make them eat. Singspiel would often leave food so you would take it back. They cannot perform without the food. With him we'd try things like feeding him little and often. Or we'd change what he was eating. That would make him curious about what was on offer. He didn't stand out to me either in his early work. He got beaten at Chester, which effectively ruled him out of the Derby. At that point we really needed to get protein into him, as he was always a nice horse to look at but did need to fill out. We ended up switching, trying things like naked oat, which has the outside removed. Anything with extra protein was worth a go.

'He got sick in Japan. He did a lot of travelling that autumn of 1996: two trips to Canada, then east. Then there was a trip to Dubai still to come. I was flown out to see him in Japan. He had stopped eating and had a temperature. He was down when I first saw him. There was another horse from Australia also being prepped for the race – Saintly, trained by Bart Cummings – who went down the same way. In Japan you are in quarantine for about twelve days, then you move on to Tokyo and have a week there before the Japan Cup itself. We both seemed to get over the problem at the same time, and the Japanese vets wanted to stop the antibiotic courses we had both been put on. The boss said to keep going. The Cummings people stopped with their course and went on ahead to Tokyo, but after arriving it wasn't long before Saintly had a relapse. Cummings then caused a bit of trouble by implying that we had received the better veterinary care. By the time we were due to travel, with the antibiotics finished, Singspiel began to pick up. On arriving in Tokyo it was clear to us that he was very much his old self. He proved that on the track.'

Pilsudski was always the daddy. 'Singspiel was never going to be as big as Pilsudski,' Scott believes. 'With him, it seemed that you just could not bottom him. When I followed Pilsudski at a canter I always liked the way he moved up the gallops. There was always a sense of more to come. With each season he just got better and better, both at home and on the track. He turned out to be something of a gentle giant. Even in his older days and in the days leading up to an important race when he'd be ready to go, he was always dead straightforward to manage at the yard, and when travelling.'

'We were told that Pilsudski had been born out in a field at stud, not in the foaling barn,' Messenger reveals. 'They brought him back in using a wheelbarrow. I remember when he was a two-year-old. The boss and me were just standing there and he walked towards us, then fell over and tripped on to his head. Hardly a show of promise, and no reason to expect much. The old man said to me, "If that is not a racehorse, then I'll pack it in." I still don't know for sure what exactly he saw to make him so sure. He just knew.'

'Terrific temperaments, the pair of them,' Scott insists. 'Big hearts and great engines. Singspiel and Pilsudski were both very good flyers, that's for sure. It can be a problem if you go with other horses – I have seen loose horses on a plane – but whenever they flew they would be ready to race in very little time, both of them.'

*

Zilzal in 1989 and King's Best eleven years later proved themselves two milers of the highest quality. Scott and Messenger had to learn their ways too. 'I got left on Zilzal one morning on the Limekilns,' Scott recalls. 'I caught the lead horses within a furlong and then finished about ten lengths ahead of the pack. And they were all winners. I looked behind me and couldn't actually believe it. The best miler, certainly, I have ever sat on in my life. King's Best really began to stand out at three. I came back from a winter holiday and I could see a big difference in him from the previous year. Soon after that I rode him up Warren Hill. That gallop often tells you a lot about them. In his case it was effortless. Joe Mercer, racing manager to the owner, Saeed Suhail, came out that morning. He said to me, "Jesus Christ, he moves really good." He wasn't a big horse but he covered a lot of ground.

'King's Best could be funny at the races, though. You wouldn't know from the gallops that he might be. Over time we realised that he needed confidence – so a nice long rein. With Zilzal, everyone would say that he was a difficult horse, but he wasn't at all. Sure, he used to sweat, but that was pretty much all he did. Maybe sometimes he was a little bit stubborn before going on to the gallops, but not much, and not very often.' With Zilzal, quality prevailed. 'I rode him quite a few times at two,' Scott continues. 'Then when we took him to Leicester as a three-year-old he was up against a Henry Cecil favourite called Belhomme. Still, I knew that this horse wouldn't stop to win. On the day we got 5–2. It felt like Christmas. Afterwards, Steve Cauthen, who was riding for Henry, got off Belhomme and said if we had run in the Guineas we'd have won that too. I think the boss knew that Zilzal was good from very early on. He could see he was sweating so, just in case it affected him mentally, he brought him along slowly. The temptation would have been to rush him. Steve Cauthen was right. He might well have won the Guineas. But I would bet that if he had, we wouldn't be talking about him now.

'He was never difficult, and by that I mean bad to handle. He needed company, so when we flew anywhere, to America for instance, we would never leave him alone. Feed-wise he could sometimes be a little fussy. But so long as, on the road, you kept him drinking to compensate for the sweating, he was absolutely fine. He was too immature to run as a two-year-old, that was all. He was a little on the weak side. But even then, once he galloped we knew we had something. He was nothing special to look at. He'd sweat on the gallops too. But people had him wrong. There was nothing bad about him at all. If he didn't sweat you'd worry. It just meant that races took a bit more out of him.'

King's Best was also prone to the sweats, Scott admits. 'We had to relax him. Anyone who rode him had to be careful.

You had to try and switch him off. Stuart and I also had to school him by taking him up to the racecourse a few times before the 2,000 Guineas. It meant extra work, but it paid off.'

'About ten days before the Guineas we started to work on building him up mentally,' Messenger says. 'We'd drive up in the evening to the racecourse in the horsebox for a couple of spins round the parade ring just to get him familiar with the surrounds. Before that we also took him up when they were racing at Newmarket and put a saddle on him, then walked him round. This got him confident about the whole parade and paddock routine. On Guineas day, he knew where he was. It was funny being at Newmarket when the racecourse was empty. The place can seem quite spooky. Obviously the place was packed on race day, though. I led him round and he seemed absolutely ready to run for his life. At least he did to me. In the middle of the parade ring there was some guy on the phone talking to his bookmaker or someone. I heard him say, "King's Best has lost it. He's got no chance." I hardly heard because we had so much in hand. King's Best was so well. We were just trying to keep a hold of him.'

For Zilzal, it was ultimately just a single season that ended with defeat in America. 'A real shame,' says Scott. 'For the Breeders' Cup Mile, they gave us permission for me to lead him down – he was like Shahrastani: he liked people around he knew – then they changed their minds. For me that cost him any chance in the race. The stable they put us in was also the worst for him, like an oven. It was still terrible when we found out that he wasn't coming back from America. I think that was hard for the whole yard. He was a great horse, but he would have been even better at four. We'd worked him out completely and knew exactly what he liked and didn't like.'

And King's Best over twelve furlongs? 'No trouble,' Messenger believes. 'A mile and a half would have been great for him. We didn't find out about twelve furlongs when he ran in the Irish Derby as he was injured in running. After that, like Zilzal in America, he never came home. An empty box in the yard when that happens is always a pretty gut-wrenching sight. In his work he would be really relaxed, and he would keep that turn of foot in reserve. With each gallop, the more he went on, the more confident he became. He'd only have got better. Plus he changed physically after the Guineas. He really filled out and became much more powerful.

'I was never surprised that King's Best had such raw ability. I rode his mother, Allegretta. I always liked him right from the start. He always looked like he'd become a proper racehorse. He got his strength up over the winter. He stood out in the spring as a three-year-old. In the days leading up to the Guineas, we'd let King's Best pick at grass after he had worked on the gallops. We had two for the Guineas that year – Misraah also ran – but of the pair King's Best became less and less interested in the grass. He just wanted to get on with the race. I remember a bird swooping down and he threw his head back at it. He was ready.'

*

Alongside all the highs over the decades, there have been lows too. 'I was in Barbados when I found out Shergar had been kidnapped in Ireland,' Scott recalls. 'I heard it on the world news, maybe even ahead of everyone at the yard. What can you say?'

'It was a big shock,' says Messenger. 'Strangely, it wasn't like it would have been today, with masses of camera and television crews. For us in Newmarket it was almost as if it was just our story. Everyone at the yard and in the town had their own ideas. We all thought that he would turn up somewhere.'

'Racing-wise, I'd thought that was it for him in September, a week before the 1981 St Leger, where he got beaten,' Scott admits. 'In the lead-up to the race he didn't blossom in his coat like he had earlier in the summer. He just didn't look like the same horse. It was partly, I think, that he had had a tough schedule. Remember that he was winning by ten lengths. If we had known at the start of the season how good he really was, he'd have been asked to win only by half a length. Those big wins are bound to take it out of a horse, even him, and any Classic is a hard race. I remember looking at him at Doncaster and thinking, "No, not today."'

'I wasn't able to tell, like Jimmy, that maybe he wasn't at his peak,' Messenger confesses. 'It was a sad day when he came back from Donny. You don't like seeing them get beaten when they are that good, whoever trains them.'

Messenger suffered himself, with Singspiel in America

for the Breeders' Cup. 'When he got injured at Hollywood Park ahead of the Breeders' Cup Turf, it was a typical misty morning at the track. You couldn't see the other side of the racecourse. I was standing with Sir Michael. We saw Singspiel gallop for half a furlong, then he disappeared into the fog. After a while, Singspiel had not reappeared. The boss turned and said to me, "He should be back here by now." At this point you are helpless. America and the Breeders' Cup is a long way to go for nothing. You should be running in one of the greatest races in the world, then you have to switch just simply to saving them.

'When they suffer a leg injury they can shatter the bone just from getting up. With Singspiel, clearly it was serious. Looking back and thinking about the vets' urgency, that is unmistakable to me now. At least we saved him for stud. I see him every year at Dalham Hall, in Newmarket, when they parade the stallions. It seems to me that they have to be careful with him. For the mares, I know he has his own little mounting block. Even today, with everything he has done and been through, he is still a gentleman. I saw Machiavellian covering a mare once. He just took off from the door and hit the poor mare at some speed. Singspiel was a bit more roses and chocolates. Then, when he gets off the mare he always makes sure he lands on his good leg.'

*

Kribensis is still thankfully safe and at the yard, as the stable's hack, and just about settled down. 'He could always pull right from his days as a two-year-old in 1986,' Messenger remembers. 'Then he broke his jaw on the stable bar. A lad walked passed and he went for him. He fell back and hit the bar with his chin. It didn't take much time for the jaw to heal, but afterwards he was even harder to hold. As a result of the break he was dead on one side of his jaw, and when the bit lodged in a certain position he wouldn't feel it at all. You could pull the reins all you liked – nothing. Everyone struggled with him, including Richard Dunwoody whenever he rode him on the gallops.'

'He was always a quirky old boy,' Scott says with a laugh. 'When they are difficult like him, you wire them up, and we did with him. Even to break in he was hard. He wouldn't lunge, and we could hardly persuade him to trot. A funny bugger. He always had a temper. It was just a streak in him. A positive of this was that it did give him a really competitive side. He would think that he knew everything. I rode him a lot on the Al Bahathri gallop before the Triumph Hurdle in 1988. Some mornings he'd be lazy, so you'd give him all his rein. Then you would do the same the next day and he'd take you, drop the lot on you and pull your arms out. He'd just mess you around. But, let's be sure about this, I saw many worse than him when I was at Boyd-Rochfort's stable. At stud these days, foals and yearlings are handled so much better. When I started we couldn't even catch some of the yearlings. Today it is totally different.'

'Schooling Kribensis was the fastest I have ever been on a horse,' Messenger insists. 'No Bombs, who was with us, was a good hurdler, but Kribensis was another matter. Steve Smith Eccles, who was the first to ride him ahead of Dunwoody, said he'd never been so fast too. He'd clear his fences by just an inch. He was clever, and always saw a stride. That was good for me. When I rode him, my eyes were usually closed!'

'His first schooling was long before anyone thought about sending him jumping,' Scott reveals. 'He got loose in the paddock and skipped over a log. The old man said, "He looks like a jumper!" It was unusual for Sheikh Mohammed to have a jumper, and in those days it was pretty unusual for him to have a four-year-old still in training. Smith-Eccles wasn't convinced at first. He didn't rate him after their first run at the racecourse. Then Mark Dwyer won on him – the Fighting Fifth at Newcastle. Afterwards, he told me, "This one is top-class."'

'Being gelded was the making of him,' Messenger believes. 'He climbed up on another colt. He was too young to know the difference between them and fillies. But that was still the end of his days as a colt. The plus was that he finally was able to concentrate on his racing. Even then you had to be careful. He was a nice horse all right. You just had to look after him in a certain way.'

'He kicked a car once,' says Scott, laughing. 'We were out on the roads one day ahead of the Champion Hurdle after his win in the Triumph. Kribensis seemed fine with this so we put a girl up on him and sent them off with some company. While he was out there he kicked out and caught

something like a saloon. I remember thinking, "Blimey."
Then this big bloke got out of the car. I thought, "I'm on the
hack so I'm in charge," and went over to try and make sure
everything was calm. I said sorry and told the man that it
was Kribensis. "Don't worry about the car," he said. "Is he
all right?" He'd backed him for Cheltenham. It's a pity he
couldn't win the Champion Hurdle for him that March as
well as the following year, when he did.'

A change of scene always helped keep Kribensis on the
road. 'He would be stabled at David Nicholson's in the build-
up to Cheltenham,' Scott recalls. 'The first time we went
down there, Dunwoody said to me, "Don't worry, Jimmy, he
won't pull up these gallops," which were straight up Cleeve
Hill. Well, he carried me all the way to the top without pulling
up. After that, Dunwoody just said, "OK, Jim, you can stay on
him for the mornings." We'd just fit in with the string. He
certainly was quite small next to those big chasers, but then
they'd see him head up the hill. He always travelled really
well, on the gallops and at the racecourse. He seemed to
mellow with age and when he was in different surrounds, so
all things considered, he was easier to manage. For him, being
at David Nicholson's was like a holiday.

'He also went to Leicester. That was after he got injured
– finished as a racehorse. Found himself turned out on a
farm. He went there because there was hunting for him after
convalescing. He healed terrific. Remember that at the time
of the injury he was close to being put down. I think the
treatment of his injury was one of the first times that vets

here used staples instead of stitches. They are commonplace now. The vets did a fantastic job. We were all just pleased that we'd be able to see him again.'

'He came back to the yard and settled in great as a hack,' Messenger recalls. 'But he was still a bit fresh. You had to make sure that he just stood off and watched. He was so used to competing that he couldn't mix in with the other horses, otherwise he would have been off. In the beginning he didn't accept it, but he got out of the habit. You'd let him pick at grass when the string was getting ready to go and hope that he didn't look up and try to join in. Funnily enough, though it was good for him at the time when he stayed at the farm in Leicester, he didn't really take to the hunting. Maybe the injury he suffered left him a bit frightened. He certainly seemed to lose a little bit of confidence. Even today, if he is ever boxed in he doesn't like it. He'll stop dead in his tracks and let the rest go on ahead before he starts again.'

'He is still on the gallops in the morning and it is just great to have him around,' says Scott. 'Winning at Cheltenham with Kribensis was probably the biggest kick I ever had out of the horses we had here. When he first went hurdling, people said, "Who is that rabbit you've got?" When he won the Triumph we paraded him round six times, and I said, "Here's your rabbit!"'

*

Working the horses out, including champion sprinter

Ajdal – that's the speciality of men like Scott, helped by Messenger. 'Ajdal always looked like being a nice horse,' Scott maintains. 'On the gallops he was like a rocket. A very good horse, easy as anything to manage, with a good temperament. I sat on him as a yearling. He was no problem at all to break in. Very straightforward, and a good feeder and traveller. Over the winter of 1986, to me he always looked like a middle-distance horse, maybe a mile and a quarter. At two, he'd work six or seven furlongs, or sometimes just five furlongs to give him a blow-out. His speed did always stand out. But galloping, he would cover some ground. He had a stride like a greyhound. His action was exceptional. A great walker. As I said, middle distances for me.'

'He wasn't wound up like speed horses sometimes are,' suggests Messenger. 'We worked him out in the end. He'd conserve his energy for that short burst on the track. I remember on the morning of the Haydock Sprint, he had that alertness which starts to come out for sprinters. He'd look around, realise that he was ready to race. Then afterwards, he'd just chill out. Always took his races well. Never the need to put him back together again after running. Definitely a sprinter.'

Compared to Ajdal, some were positively nightmarish. 'I worked with one who had suffered a really bad journey from Ireland when travelling by plane to Newmarket,' Scott recalls. 'Smashed his head, which left a hole at the pole. It took us a month to get a bridle near him, let alone on him. The hole from his smash made him very wary of anything near his head. We had to tie him out with two ropes to get the bridle on. We began by leaving a headpiece on him at night so that he would get used to that. But the bridle was only the start of the difficulties. Once we got one of those on it still took three of us to get a saddle on. Very accident-prone too. One morning we were on our way to the gallops. There was a hole in the road, with a digger and a work crew with picks and shovel. He still didn't see it, and fell into the hole. He also broke down very badly. Went over the carcass of a dead rabbit on the gallops. The vet eventually found a slither of bone from the carcass in his tendon, and some of this had been carried round his system by his bloodstream. As a result he picked up a really nasty infection. It was a freak accident. On top of everything, he also had bad kidneys. Never drank ordinary water. He needed the natural minerals, so we would collect water for him from a stream. Would you believe he won a hatful of races?

'We've had a few. At Sir Michael's there was a filly who would just sit down on you. Once, when she went down, she put her head through some sheep railings and it got stuck. We still landed a right touch on her debut. She didn't drop me either. Of course, I've been dropped a few times over the years. There was one who dropped everyone, a colt. He got loose and tried to cover the statue of Hyperion in Newmarket. Then we had his full brother. With him, the joke was that no one could catch him. Whenever we got anyone new to the stable, we'd always say, "Tie him up, would you?" They'd be stuck for an hour.'

'In a funny sort of way, the best riders actually have to partner the worst horses,' Messenger reflects. 'If they are good, you can actually put up anyone to ride them. The thing about good horses is that they are so well balanced. They don't get those cuts and grazes. They have the action. They're not weak, they're true athletes. The disappointments are the ones with the talent but who don't have the wheels on properly. They are sometimes just not up to training. At least in a yard like Sir Michael's, with such good horses going for big races, there are always good times, all being well, around the corner. That's what picks me up. You can then put everything behind you.'

CHAPTER EIGHT
LISA JACKSON

*Flagship Uberalles, and the rise
of Philip Hobbs*

Lisa Jackson blames – if that is the right word – her father that she ended up as head girl at Philip Hobbs's yard. One summer in the mid-1980s, Richard Burge took his teenage daughter to what was the local stable. He had a long-standing love of the game and watched avidly on television every Saturday. She shared his passion. A few point-to-point excursions – 'thoroughbred horses were absolutely beautiful' – and a trip to Hobbs's Minehead base just a few miles up the road from home seemed a natural progression for her. The plan was that a summer working there with horses would be potentially helpful to young Lisa in fulfilling her apparent ambition to become a mounted policewoman. Instead, Jackson found her true calling.

Back then at the yard there were only around 30 horses, compared to the three-figure string of her head girl years a decade later. The pay was not unadjacent to £60 to £70 a week, which, after driving lessons and some keep for the folks at home, left maybe a tenner. Moreover, when Jackson started the ratio of boys to girls was something like three to one against the better sex. Today, the Hobbs yard is roughly a 50–50 split. Jackson looks back on those years with a big, happy smile. Her own progress mirrored the yard's upward curve. 'At the start I was absolutely useless,' she says. 'Always just tried to ask what was going on, followed the ones who did know around all day.'

By the time Flagship Uberalles arrived from Noel Chance and became her pride and joy, Jackson was the match of any horseman. She nurtured the Queen Mother Champion Chaser back to his very best. She was once carted by Rooster Booster, but she can claim a major role in shaping that tearaway into a Champion Hurdler. Clifton Beat before them, in 1995, gave her and owner Des O'Connor a first ticket to Cheltenham for the Triumph Hurdle, and Kibreet – who, unlike In Contrast, never bit her – was her first Festival winner. The Grand Annual Chase of 1996 fulfilled a dream dating back to that first visit chez Hobbs.

At Cheltenham, Flagship's Queen Mother Champion Chase win in 2002 is Jackson's standout day, followed closely by Rooster Booster's Festival of 2003. In Contrast's Champion Hurdle was no less important to her for coming, as it did, at Ayr, and it was some compensation for the nasty bruising he gave her. Collectively they all helped offset the sadness of mornings like the one which claimed Farmer Jack just 48 hours before a live chance in the 2005 Cheltenham

Gold Cup. Or the afternoon in January 2000 when Dr Leunt suffered a fatal racecourse injury at the same track. For three or four terrible days such as these, Jackson reckons she has had fifteen worth relaying to any children and grandchildren.

If they ever ask Jackson about career choices she could well impart the sort of cunning that served her well back at the start of her gainful employment. 'After my GCSEs, I had enough qualifications to join the police force. I was already tall enough. At the recruitment centre they told me, "Better wait until you are a little older." The police prefer that. It meant that I could pacify my parents. "I'll sign up in due course," I said. Never had the slightest intention!' Hobbs's faith in Jackson was a vindication of her chosen path. 'I didn't think I could be head girl at 26 – not experienced enough,' Jackson admits. 'It was only a few years earlier that I had to be shown how to put on a saddle. Philip said, "Try for a few months, and we'll see." He wanted to promote from within. He had confidence in me, and that gave me confidence. Philip's wife Sarah, too. Always played a very big part – young at heart and knows how to enjoy herself. She rides out every day. With her it's not always about the horses. She'll ask what films are any good, what you did at the weekend. Philip and Sarah talk to you as equals. They know that without the staff, the yard just wouldn't work.'

These days, Jackson can laugh at her strength of conviction during that first summer at Hobbs's Minehead yard. 'Everyone warned me, "Don't work in a stable – long hours, poor pay and no job satisfaction." Right about the first two, definitely; wrong about the last one. I loved it so much. I spent the six weeks of my holiday there working for nothing and after that was completely attached to the horses I had been asked to look after. Then there was the chance of being paid as well. I just didn't want to go back to school. I'd taken my GCSEs at fifteen and had done quite well. I was due to go back to school for A- levels. After that summer I told everyone that this was it for me. I didn't need anything like clothes, really, as I'd just be mucking out all the time. Even when I worked for free as a schoolgirl – health and safety wouldn't allow me the run of the place now! – I felt lucky. The way I saw it, I was just privileged to sit on a racehorse.'

*

Flagship Uberalles' arrival signalled the big time. 'At the time we were already a successful yard,' Jackson recalls. 'We had hundreds of winners, but we lacked the real superstar for the Champion Hurdle, the Gold Cup. We had no Rooster Booster to speak of at Minehead yet. Flagship had the potential to be something special. We were all extremely excited. A fantastic horse. Always liked him. Even though we never liked to see one of ours beaten, you had to accept that he was superb.

'The Champion Chase he won in 2002 was one of the best days of my life. Nerve-racking, too. We were still looking for that big winner – a championship race. This added to the pressure, for the yard. Plus all the locals were rooting for him. You know how good your horse is and that he's fit and well, but you don't know for sure how good the rest are. I can't say I enjoyed the last couple of weeks before the race. My worst fear was that he would disappoint and we'd have no answers as to why. Before the race I was pathetic. I smoked furiously. Then during the race I just walked off and hid by a BT van. I am glad I did. He just never travelled. Richard Johnson gave him a great ride. I couldn't hear the commentary, but then I heard the crowd roar so I ran to the grass lawn in front of the grandstand at Cheltenham to see what was happening. I think I ran up the hill faster than even he did. After that I was on a high for about six weeks. We had runners the next day, obviously, but I had to go out that night. Then we had a big party at the weekend.

'I was on holiday when we first learnt that Flagship was coming. Apparently, Philip came into the yard and said that the owners, the Krysztofiaks, were going to have a look round. I think they were also considering some others – Henrietta Knight, for one. They wanted to see the yards before deciding where to send Flagship. The owners had a bit of a reputation before they came to the yard, so I was a bit nervous looking after him. It obviously helped that Flagship won the Tingle Creek on his first run, then won the Queen Mother.

'I have to say I was a little disappointed with him the first time I rode him. He didn't move at all well. He had problems, and I thought, "This isn't going to happen."

Basically, he had no muscle behind the saddle, nothing, and he had hock and joint problems. He simply wasn't the best of movers. He was very laid back too. It wasn't the plan that I would ride him from day one. I already had horses I rode out every day. I also didn't know if I could accept the responsibility. What would happen if he wasn't fit enough? My fault. But circumstances meant that I sat on him on that first day. After that, I stayed there.

'Mentally, the move was the best thing for Flagship. He was a wise old boy and he seemed to have lost his enthusiasm. Maybe he was thinking, "Why should I do this any more?" We did so much work with him. Instead of just going on the normal all-weather gallops with him, we'd take him out on grass. One of the first decisions was not to train him on the wood chip. I would take him out through fields, up hills, trotting and getting him to use himself and his muscles. I would trot on him diagonally, like in dressage. I'd be out on my own for over an hour. Philip would ask, "What did you do today?" It was only when Flagship started his fast work that he took more of an interest. For me, it was great. Riding him every day around beautiful countryside, trying things that weren't routine at all. Before long you could see that it was working. Instead of taking twenty minutes to warm up before you could attempt anything strenuous, he'd only need five. He was happy, and couldn't wait to get out there. He'd buck and kick with excitement. He was so well behaved – a gentleman. You'd put your children on him.

'Like any good horse, he had his ways. He refused to go into the swimming-pool. At the time it was a real shame. Mary Bromiley, the back specialist who looked after him and who knew all of his problems, suggested we swim him. We had a pool, so great. Overall, 90 per cent go in no problem. A few like to have a look or may need a bit of encouragement, but generally there's no trouble at all. He wasn't having any of it. Went berserk. Maybe it was the enclosed space: access to the pool was a narrow alleyway. We only ever tried once with him. It was obvious that it wasn't going to happen and he'd have hurt himself. At the time it was disappointing, but we were at least making progress elsewhere. In the end, we took him to the local beach about two miles from the yard. I'd take him down in the horsebox with Village King, his travelling companion. The idea was to wade him, to get the sea water on his muscles.

'You have to accept that you cannot always win them over. You also couldn't clip Flagship. He'd hear the sound and get into a huge panic. He would have to be sedated otherwise he'd be climbing up and all over his box. He didn't like any attention to his teeth either. Most horses don't have a problem with that at all. I looked after another horse called Gaysun. Adored him, but he was a savage. Being with him was like being with Flagship: you have to establish what will annoy them, and what you can get away with.'

*

Rooster Booster joined Flagship Uberalles at Cheltenham championship level. A Polytrack gallop made the difference. 'Rooster Booster seems like he has been with us for a lifetime,' says Jackson. 'He's not been a horse in the news for ever. The reason for that is that he matured very late. He was also only belatedly trained on a Polytrack surface. It was laid for the season 2002/03, when he won the Champion Hurdle. He never ran on the Flat. But he has always been one of those who doesn't seem to move that well. In the morning he'd look stiff, and he always pulled muscles easily. This made him very difficult to train. The Polytrack was much easier for him.

'I only ever rode him myself a couple of times. On the first occasion, all fine. Second time, he was very fresh, back from holiday. The plan was once up the wood chip in the days before the Polytrack. After having been laid off for a few months and fresh from having had no exercise the lads joked, "You won't hold him." They were right. We went up the wood chip a great deal faster than planned. The final stretch is very stiff, but he got to the top all right. Luckily they do know when to stop. Good job, as we might still be going otherwise. He was so strong, a girl couldn't really ride him. He was very uptight. He could bolt at any time, even with professional jockeys. Highly strung, almost nervous. If you went into his box for something a bit unusual he'd flip out in a way that was quite scary. If you had to give him an injection or something like that, he'd be a bit of a shite, if I am honest. I don't think that they were moods as such. He was just highly strung. To ride him, one day he was fine, the next he would just go.'

Rooster Booster was just biding his time. 'With the Polytrack, he changed physically and grew into a much bigger, stronger horse,' Jackson continues. 'He came into himself at nine and ten, instead of seven or eight. It wasn't that apparent. A decent handicapper, maybe not good enough for the Champion Hurdle. Then he won the County, and he had nowhere else to go. Even then we still weren't sure if he was good enough. At the time we didn't have anything to go on, really. I just hoped. On the day, my confidence wobbled. I thought, "He's just a nice horse." In fact, we all just hoped.

'Afterwards, I think everyone was surprised at how much he seemed to have improved. Winning the Champion Hurdle was another step up for the yard – tremendous. Looking back now, that March Rooster Booster was unbeatable. The party was on Sunday. It was a joint party as One Knight had won the SunAlliance. We all got very drunk and talked about how great the race was and how good Rooster Booster and One Knight were. Richard Johnson was there, of course. Not one of the workers, if you understand, but if we have a staff party he's there! He comes down when he is asked to school the likes of Rooster. His real work is at the racecourse. He is very good after a horse has run. Brilliant at giving his opinion of the horse to the lad or lass looking after him. The boss left the party early. He usually does. He has to phone 300 owners and be up by six a.m. He likes to read the *Racing Post* and get settled before the phone starts to ring at seven in the morning. Another day at the yard.'

*

Clifton Beat, Kibreet and In Contrast made Jackson into a Cheltenham Festival regular. Horses of this calibre also brought pressure. 'When I was looking after Gaysun,' Jackson reflects, 'racing was always so relaxed. We'd go to places like Stratford and further west. I got as much pleasure from those excursions as anywhere. At Cheltenham, it is very different. When Flagship ran badly at the Festival everyone would want to know why. Unfortunately they cannot talk to us. They have their off days like the rest of us.

'In general, there is less time now than when I started with Philip. All the extra pressure of being a top yard. In my early days we looked after three and were able to exercise them for over an hour; today it's maybe a more concentrated 40 minutes, after a ten-minute warm-up. An American barn went up over a decade ago, and there were more boxes every season. Then a few years ago Philip built a second new barn. We had people wanting to send us horses before we'd even got the boxes built up.

'I always wanted to look after a Festival winner. I was in awe of the occasion. I had never been before I started working for Philip. As a family we've never been very far out of Taunton. My first time at Cheltenham was with Clifton Beat for the Triumph Hurdle in 1995. Oh my God – I'm taking a horse to the Festival! In those days it was on the Thursday. A runner on Gold Cup day! We actually had three in the race: Clifton Beat, Greenback, and dear old Dr Leunt, who I ended up looking after. Walking round that paddock, with the amphitheatre which is so different from every other racecourse, I was so thrilled just to be there. It was like being on a different level.

'With Kibreet, I ended up looking after him because another horse I looked after left on the same day. He was eight when he arrived. He had run in the Arkle. Gerald Cottrell, who trained him before us, was pretty upset to see him leave. They thought quite a lot of him. He was such good fun. Jumping, he was a pleasure to watch. I rode him pretty much every day. He loved life. He'd be walking in the yard, then for no obvious reason he would let out this squeal. He was like a dolphin. He would do this quite often. But there was never anything naughty. No bucking or kicking out, just a squeal of delight. He'd walk really slowly. He'd hold up the whole string if he was at the front.

'Working him, he was like a machine. Nothing could get near him, even horses off the Flat. I'd never ridden anything so fast. He was keen and strong, but Kibreet would never run away with you, like Rooster Booster. He just didn't want any horse to pass him. Kibby never wanted to be headed. He would always fight back if a horse came upsides him. The trouble with that was that he could disappoint other horses, but what can you do with him when he is such a tryer? You cannot disappoint him either. He had such a high action you could pick him out on the gallops miles off. Jumping, sometimes the jockeys would leave sideways out of the saddle. He was just so exuberant – legs everywhere.'

Off the Flat, they usually took the Rooster Booster course, up the Polytrack gallop. 'The drill is no different. When they come off the Flat they haven't had much holiday so they are roughed off for a bit. They are also cut – I never know what to say when kids ask me about that – which can take a bit of getting used to, and they can be off for three months. Some change a bit after the operation. One of the problems with colts is that they are around mares. They go on the Polytrack to adjust, like Rooster. A lot of Flat horses have just had too much racing to stay jumping beyond eight or nine, compared to horses bred for jumping. Off the Flat, they can bring problems before you even start. Polytrack helps greatly.

'Clifton Beat was off the Flat, from the Ramsdens. A lovely, keen, enthusiastic horse. They aren't all like that. But he was straightforward. It was obvious from riding him that he was very fast. His problem was that he just didn't stay two miles, certainly not at Cheltenham, though he was fifth in the Triumph. Aintree, nice and flat, was his track. He was placed in a big handicap hurdle on Grand National day twice in a row, and in a novice chase there.

'With In Contrast – or Inkey, to me – I try to tell everyone that there is no difference between the Scottish Champion

Hurdle and the one at Cheltenham. Inkey just oozed class. He knew he was a bit special. Came from Ireland as a four-year-old, with a pretty good reputation. He was a replacement for Dr Leunt, who I also looked after. He won the Racing Post Chase. Devastating when he died at Cheltenham. But I did think when I first set eyes on Inkey that he wasn't that special considering he obviously cost a bit of money. And he was so miserable – ears back. Not nice at all for the first couple of weeks. He was just a miserable bugger. He never really cheered up. He got used to you and vice versa. You didn't go grooming him for two hours, or hang off his neck and kiss him like Flagship. You just went in, did your stuff, and left. He only bit me once, but when he did it was hard. I was just brushing him and had stopped to talk with someone. He wasn't having that. It really hurt; it's the shock as much as anything. Only bruising, and not a return to casualty, which is where I ended up the first time I was bitten by a mare. I knew I had to have Inkey tied up, and have a head collar on. I wouldn't even contemplate going into his box without him being tied up, as I'd get in his way, and the other way round. I still loved him, though. It's just his character. He won his bumpers so well. It was like he had sprouted wings. I thought, "This is the horse I have been waiting for all my life." Everyone was saying, "He'll win a Champion Hurdle." Then you start to worry. The ones you have to look after you'd just be happy enough to win something at Newton Abbot.'

*

'Farmer Jack's death was absolutely devastating. He was with us for just two seasons, but one of my best friends, Amy, looked after him. We shared a flat together and were very close. That probably made it worse. She was riding him at the time and I was in the pair following behind. He went up the wood chip once – fine, no problem. He almost got to the top a second time. Then he just seemed to stumble. What happened was instantaneous. He dived to the right. I thought maybe he had tripped. Then I realised that wasn't what had happened. He fell into the bank and Amy took a really heavy tumble. I pulled up and jumped off. He was dead by the time I got to him. The vets were called immediately. Of course, there was nothing any of them could do. When horses die on the gallops, they are taken almost straight away to the local kennels. It was terrible, as it was in the week of the Gold Cup, and he had a chance for sure. The worst thing is that there is this empty box in the yard.

'When any horse dies there is always an empty feeling. You have an involvement with all of them. But Dr Leunt was different because he was one of mine. When you have been riding and grooming them, then it really hurts. But you have to accept it otherwise you don't stay in the game. As you get older you look at life differently. You know that things still happen to people. But in your teens it is very hard to accept.

'I was there with Dr Leunt at Cheltenham. I didn't see anything, though. He hadn't run a bad race. He finished behind Looks Like Trouble. I began to walk out to collect him. You see the quad bikes set off and your first thought is, "If there's a problem, I just hope it's not mine." Then you realise that yours has not come back to the unsaddling area. With Dr Leunt, at that point I knew. You want to wait and see. You also want to help if there is anything you can do. I started walking up, then I saw Andrew Thornton, who rode him, walking back with his saddle. I knew for sure then. He explained that he had had a heart attack. How brave he was. You just want a private moment. People are concerned; the crowd is devastated too. But you really want to be alone and have a cry.'

*

With Flagship Uberalles, Jackson dealt with two owners: the Krysztofiaks and, of course, J.P. McManus, who bought the gelding and was rewarded with success in the BMW Chase at Punchestown in April 2003. If things had worked out differently, Jackson herself would have been owner number three. 'I always think of the horses in my care as my own,' she says. 'I know they're not, but you feel very possessive. With Flagship Uberalles, I actually had the chance to take him after he retired. Frank Berry, J.P. McManus's racing manager, spoke to Philip about whether I would like to have him. I had been in a complete panic when Flagship was sold to J.P. McManus. A real shock to me. I was on holiday in America. We'd been to New York – fantastic! – and Las Vegas. We arrived back at Heathrow and the front of that day's *Racing Post* said "SOLD!" I rang the yard straight away. I was told, "Don't worry, he isn't going anywhere. He's staying with us."

'He was a fantastic-looking horse – tall, handsome, the sort you see walking round the paddock who always catches racegoers' eyes. A really beautiful head. He really stands out. When he arrived at the yard he was turned out straight away with the rest of the string. In a field near the yard. The stable is part of Crown Estates so there is plenty of space. I went out to visit him, to have a look at the new boy. I had no trouble finding him. I wanted to look after him from day one. Being head girl gave me a little bit of an advantage. "You've been here ten times longer than anyone else," I was told, "so it's only fair!" And the owners wanted a girl to look after him. They knew, as everyone does, that a horse will get looked after better by one of us.

'We always knew that the Queen Mother in 2005 would probably be his last race. In fact it was a bit last-minute that he ran. Then, when he disappointed, J.P. waited a couple of weeks before announcing that he was going to be retired. That was what I wanted. He had reached a grand old age and there was always the danger that something would happen to him. If he got injured in a race when he was just out the back, without any chance of winning – what a waste.

'I know he was never my horse. I have still been over to see him at Martinstown, J.P.'s stud in Ireland. They don't belong to you, but you can struggle to feel any different. I was just missing him. I rang Frank Berry and said, "It's been six weeks or so. Do you mind if I drop in?" It was no problem. J.P. loves his horses and is genuinely concerned about how they all are. He understood. His horses all go back to his place in Ireland over the summer. They are completely checked out by the vets there for any damage or problems. They are turned out in a lovely environment. Obviously he has a lot of money. But even so, not many owners would incur the cost of flying all their horses home for the summer for a break.

'Owning Flagship would have been a dream. I was so touched by the offer. But I just didn't have anywhere to put him.'

CHAPTER NINE

IAN WILLOWS

Luca Cumani's best,
the world over

Ian Willows claims not to remember dates, save his birthday, and 1066. Having travelled the world shipping horses for Luca Cumani, he has a much clearer recollection of places. Racing-wise, however, he really should be able to recall 1976. That was the year when he joined Bedford House stables, once Cumani had taken out a licence. Apart from an interview with the sales company Tattersalls, Willows has never looked beyond the place since. 'Luca talked me out of that move, said I wouldn't like it at all,' Willows recalls with a laugh. Certainly there would have been much less flying the flag had Willows taken the Tattersalls shilling. As Cumani's head travelling man he has experienced many moments yielding both national pride and air miles.

Before Cumani, Willows worked for Fred Winter senior and his son John after his own father packed in the pub he ran. Birthright denied, Willows minor had to find

alternative employment. After Winter, he hit the road for
Cumani, travelling the best of Bedford House to Italy,
France and Ireland. Japan, North America and beyond
followed. On early excursions to Milan, Willows met a
young Frankie Dettori. The teenager would fetch the coffees
by scooter. In time he ended up at Bedford House too.
Tolomeo was the maiden voyage statesside. The journey
with Willows to the Arlington Million in 1983 broke new
ground for many of Cumani's training generation, also
based in Newmarket. By the days of Barathea, the road to
America was well travelled. His success in winning the 1994
Breeders' Cup Mile at Churchill Downs is, probably,
Willows's career highlight after a disappointment twelve
months earlier at Santa Anita.

Falbrav is a more recent first-class global traveller. Good
as gold on the road, according to Willows, but an altogether
different prospect on the gallops or in the horsebox, once
finally persuaded in. A Japan Cup winner on arrival, the colt
still managed to enhance his reputation with wins in the
Eclipse, International and Queen Elizabeth II Stakes, in
Cumani's care, and chaperoned by Willows. 'A monster,'
reckons Willows, but rewarding. 'Winning is what you work
for, strive for, and what you travel for,' he maintains. 'When
you win abroad, there's a certain extra satisfaction – some
patriotic pride, and pride in Newmarket. A good job done.'

At home, Willows has accompanied two Derby winners
down the M11 from Newmarket to Epsom: Kahyasi in 1988
and High-Rise a decade later. His other domestic Classic

journey was to Doncaster with Commanche Run for the St Leger in 1984, which took Lester Piggott past Frank Buckle's longstanding record of 27 domestic Classic winners. Once he'd poached the saddle, Piggott had Willows to thank for a smooth run up north. Likewise, owners such as the late Gerald Leigh have reason to be grateful for the safe transportation of their pride-and-joys. Willows, in turn, is honoured to have been associated with the likes of Leigh's Markofdistinction and Gossamer, a Classic winner in Ireland. Markofdistinction's Queen Elizabeth II Stakes win in 1990 was Dettori's first Group One winner, and on the day a double of the highest rank.

Paddy Rudkin, head lad at Henry Cecil's when Cumani served there as assistant, brokered Willows's arrival at Bedford House. Willows thinks now that the interview he arranged was probably a formality. 'Luca back then?' Willows chuckles. 'Young, free and single. Luca makes everyone think about things, and he keeps feet on the ground. Always very serious and dedicated to his work. He hasn't changed an awful lot, really. I think getting married and having a family was good for him. Otherwise he's not that much different now than back then. A little more English, maybe. But the Italian is still there. He's proud of that. And aware of the shortcomings [a temper, apparently] that come with being Italian!'

At home and on the road there have been the inevitable disappointments, over and above a few private setbacks on the golf course. During Willows's time with Cumani, the

Aga Khan has twice withdrawn horses from Bedford House, and High-Rise was reposted to Dubai after Cumani had delivered the colt's owners, the Maktoum family, the top-ranked Derby. Good days, though – thanks again to Commanche Run, this time over ten furlongs – have far outweighed the bad. And that's both at home and abroad.

Willows's primary reason for feeling grateful towards Cumani for the last four decades is probably his boss's instinct for a tilt at the biggest races, wherever they may be. 'You start planning in your mind six or seven days before you leave, and draw up a list of what you'll need,' Willows explains. 'The boss decides the travel schedule – we have a system based on the recovery rate for the horse – then you go on ahead. When you arrive, the runners can be a bit flat. So you have to build them back up.' Willows has thrived on that extra responsibility when the Cumani stable's on the move. Abroad, he says, you have to be Luca's eyes and ears. And be prepared for all sorts, while travelling hopefully.

*

'Over the years, we've certainly had the odd scare,' Willows confesses. 'It was quite hairy flying to Gulfstream Park with a filly called Red Slippers, owned by Sheikh Mohammed. She was due to run in a support race on Breeders' Cup Day that year, 1992. I was in the back of the plane with Nicky Vaughan from John Gosden's, who everyone knows is the footballer David Platt's brother-in-law. We hit some turbulence and had a sudden drop in altitude. When you fly horses, it is very different to when you are travelling as a passenger. Upstairs in first class, even in economy, you wouldn't notice as everything is bolted down. In cargo, the crates in the aircraft lift off the floor. In our case, all the dust shot out from underneath as they came down. The smell afterwards was like the inside of a Hoover bag, really musty and choking. Red Slippers hit her head on the ceiling and cut herself. Frightened the life out of Nicky.

'Coming back from America with Free Guest – she won the old Extel Handicap at Goodwood in 1984 – was also pretty testing. For some reason we couldn't get back direct to Newmarket. So we flew to Paris instead. Then we were sent to Longchamp overnight. The next day there was racing there. We were moved on again. In the end we had to pick up a plane at a local airport which was full of yearlings coming from America, following us over. Finally, on the way home we were told on board by the crew that there was a problem with the plane's flaps. During the flight we were made to sit at the back of the plane, and for landing we had to belt up a distance from the horses. The descent seemed to take for ever. Then, without the flaps to soften the ride, we smashed down on to the runway. The teeth were certainly rattled. All the horses went down too, and then came back up again. The consensus among the crew was that it had been a really good landing, all things considered. The pilot did incredibly well to slow up on the ground without flaps. I suppose that, in the circumstances, any landing was pretty good.

'All the horses we travel have their own way. You probably know Zomaradah these days as the dam of Dubawi. When she was trained by Luca it was very challenging to ship her. She still ran in an awful lot of places – Italy, Canada, America – despite having her own way about flights. In her day, going to Canada meant quite a delay at the airport. You were always carted right across the tarmac to a big hangar and made to wait there for what seemed like an age. By the time she was released from the hangar she was awash with sweat. But she was like Tolomeo – great powers of recovery. Her condition always dipped but she drank and ate well. We made sure that she put back on everything she lost in transit.'

Tolomeo's trip in 1983 was a journey into the unknown. 'As far as I can remember it was our first time, or at least our first successful time,' Willows recalls. 'Tolomeo had been second in the Guineas, so we knew we had a good one. The Million was his pinnacle. I remember walking back in front of the crowds after winning. The Yanks weren't too pleased because he beat John Henry, who was, of course, a local hero. They struggled to accept that. John McCririck was out there with us and had made things worse. He caused a furore before the race by saying that US jockeys were butchers. An American trainer – I think he was called Johnny Campo, which was a great name – took the greatest offence and said, basically, that European runners had no chance in the race.

'Tolomeo was a pretty good traveller. Chicago that

summer was exceptionally hot. I have been to a good few Arlington Millions over the years but that time was the most hot and humid ever. What made Tolomeo exceptional were his powers of recovery after the long journey. After travelling, every horse will drop down a peg or two physically. Are horses aware that they are in a different place? I don't know about that. But wherever they go they certainly get dehydrated in transit. Ideally, you need a nice steady recovery to come back from that and the effects of travel as a whole. Tolomeo seemed to bounce back.

'It is hard to gauge what precise effect the heat had on Tolomeo when we arrived. I'm not even sure if the temperature made it harder for him to recover from the journey. Take the example of Shamshir, who won the Fillies' Mile at Ascot in 1990. As a three-year-old, she went to Toronto for the E.P. Taylor Stakes when it was pretty mild and she still developed pleurisy and a form of shipping fever, probably because her barn was quite damp. She became quite ill. Overall, I remember that Tolomeo just seemed quite amenable about being in Chicago. He didn't need a racetrack pony for company, or any special handling. What confirmed his good recovery was a great blow-out before the race. He was really impressive. Leo Hughes rode him. He wasn't a work rider as such, but he was an excellent stable man and a great judge of a horse. He had looked after a lot of good ones with Harry Wragg. After Leo had ridden Tolomeo we knew for sure that he was in good form.

'We went in advance of Luca, who arrived three or four

days before the race. We had a head start. Looking back, it was lucky we went with such a good traveller for our first time. It was a voyage into the unknown, the year before the Breeders' Cup started. I seem to remember there were no scheduled flights to Chicago – to charter a plane would have been way too expensive – so we went via Paris and Charles de Gaulle airport. We were accompanied by a flying groom who always did the Chicago run, so there was a specialist to hand. He helped us out a great deal.

'Things haven't changed much since then. Today we travel with our own feed whenever possible. In Japan, you have to send it ahead a couple of months before the race so you can test the feed, and they confiscate your medicine chest on arrival. Anything they don't like they take off you and replace with what they consider to be their alternative.

'Of the whole Arlington trip, the trickiest part was probably that we couldn't get the winner's garland – a mass of flowers embroidered on to material – over Tolomeo's head. It was a huge thing, very heavy and very bright colours. He could be a nervous horse, the sort who might spook at something like that. Funnily enough, returning home was quite low key. I thought it might be a big thing, but it wasn't in the end. At least not outside the yard. It certainly was to us.'

*

Willows has a double hand of winning Derby experience, thanks to the Aga Khan's Kahyasi, and High-Rise, owned by the Maktoum family. 'With both Kahyasi and High-Rise we knew we were going to Epsom with a chance,' recalls Willows. 'In fact, more so probably with High-Rise. John Francome always said that Kahyasi had fantastic balance. That's obviously crucial round Epsom. You get these great big horses, the Dubai Millenniums of this world, who fall down the hill. Prior to the Derby, our two both showed that they could travel down the hill by winning the Lingfield Derby Trial.

'For Kahyasi, who ran when the Derby was on a Wednesday, we went the day before, just to get settled in. The traffic wasn't as bad in those days and it was a Tuesday so you'd have a good enough run. For High-Rise in 1998, the Derby had been moved to Saturday. That meant heading south on the day, leaving very early. Otherwise you hit the Friday-afternoon traffic on the M25. A real pain.

'Luca always takes potential runners to different gallops for something special, like round the wrong way on the Limekilns. Not before a trial like the race at Lingfield, but before the Derby itself. You go into the trial to find out if you have got a shot. Then you prepare. Neither of those horses ever did a stunning gallop that made us think, "OK, we're in business here." But we knew there were grounds for optimism. The pair of them didn't need much work. In fact, High-Rise didn't seem to do much work at all. Luca would gallop him once a month with good horses, and the rest of the time with ordinary ones. I've actually always been convinced that the reason High-Rise struggled with

Godolphin after he left us for his four-year-old season was that they didn't have the bad horses we had to work with him on the gallops.

'They both had great temperaments. High-Rise and Kahyasi were a couple of cool dudes. In their days, both were stabled at our satellite yard. That's the small one down on the Snailwell Road. Commanche Run was stabled there too. It has always been lucky for us and it's also quiet down there, very serene almost. The stables are not what you would call luxurious, as they are big old stud boxes and quite ancient. But the horses can get their heads over the doors and look around. In the afternoons, I'd imagine that's very pleasant for them, and helps keep them calm. Of the two, High-Rise was probably the most mellow. At Godolphin the following year, we saw him with cross nosebands and the like which to us was very strange as he'd always been very manageable, pretty relaxed. Maybe he was missing the Snailwell calm.'

Kahyasi's Derby in 1988 was Cumani's first. 'Kahyasi was always a nice horse,' Willows says. 'He won at the Rowley Mile and we knew he was good. At Newmarket, he was strongly fancied. The boss would have seen a good few Derby winners around the place so he'd have known what he was looking for. These days he always jokes that he trained a Derby winner twelve years after taking out his licence, which is less time than it took Henry Cecil! He has always been quite competitive like that. On the day, though, Kahyasi wasn't anything like favourite. Red Glow, trained by Geoff Wragg, was really fancied. One of our old lads – I forget his name – who had moved on from Luca's looked after him. We had the old Aga Khan green and chocolate colours, and Doyoun, who had won the 2,000 Guineas, was in the modern green and red design. The lad leading him up on the day was a fellow called Andy Keates. These days he's Frankie Dettori's driver. He's certainly not wearing his Ever Ready sponsor's jerkin from Derby Day any more. The richest man in Newmarket now. He bought a house on the back of Kahyasi and carried on from there.

'I didn't come back with him after the Derby. I stayed down at Epsom as the race then was on a Wednesday. We had a Coronation Cup runner so I missed out on quite a journey. The blacksmith hitched a ride back, along with a bottle of whisky for company. Naturally enough, there was a big welcoming committee when they got home. They all fell out of the box.'

But with both the Aga Khan and High-Rise, disappointments lay ahead. 'After Epsom,' Willows continues, 'Kahyasi struggled to win the Irish Derby in a way that was a real contrast with Epsom. I think the reason for this was that in the race he was struck into on the outside near his cannonbone, in the process of beating Insan, trained by Paul Cole for Fahd Salman. The end result of this was that Kahyasi was never really the same horse. Before and after the race we'd been staying at one of the Aga's yards in Ireland. Luca doesn't like giving antibiotics to fit horses, but after the race the Aga's vets came and had a look. By this time the guv'nor and His Highness had flown off and I couldn't contact them – there were no mobile phones in those days. Anyway, I said, "No antibiotics," but I was outmuscled on the treatment. They nearly killed him. He lost all his condition and looked an absolute mess. He was always quite a boney horse, but after the treatment his frame was like a triangle. I don't think he ran again until September.

'The switch of High-Rise, who ran for Sheikh Mohammed Obaid Al Maktoum when he was with us, to Godolphin was hard to take. It is always pretty devastating to lose a good horse. With High-Rise, it was shattering. In the 1998 Arc he didn't have the easiest of runs, and we were all set to go to the Breeders' Cup after that. Then we got the call to say, no, he was off to Dubai. That was awful news. When that happens you usually learn from the jungle telegraph. I think I might have gone into the boss's office to ask about the plans for America only to find out there had been a change. The boss was as disappointed as the rest of us.

'When the Aga's horses left the yard at the end of 1999, it was the second time for us. He had also pulled out in 1991 after the Oaks in 1989 when Aliysa was disqualified. This time it was about positive tests for our runners. The Aga Khan wanted a number of changes to procedures at the yard which the boss believed he implemented. He was convinced that he was in the right. In all, pretty messy.'

*

Before the brace of Derby wins, in 1984 Bedford House had a first Classic winner in Commanche Run. Lester Piggott poached the ride from Darrel McHargue. Then he stayed in the saddle for a highly successful ten-furlong campaign at four.

'George Dunwoody, Richard's father, looked after Commanche Run,' Willows recalls. 'George had trained in Ireland so he knew his horses all right. Commanche Run was a real gent, and a lovely horse to look after. George was very proud of him, except that he never led the horse up at the races. I think maybe he felt that, as an ex-trainer himself, he'd leave that to someone else. So I went up with him to Doncaster instead of George.

'It was probably only Lester Piggott's brilliance that got Commanche Run home that day, after all the fuss about him taking the ride from Darrel. I'm not saying for sure Darrel wouldn't have won the St Leger, or any of the races that followed for that matter, but Lester made sure he did. When he won the St Leger, Commanche Run wasn't really right. A week before the race he stumbled on his knees and took all the skin off. It took a lot of work at the yard – and worry – just to get him to the race in a fit state. He certainly wasn't himself at all. The concern was that the grazes would become infected. He had to have medication. Plus, he needed extra exercise and trotting to stop the knees stiffening up. They say horses don't feel the pain of an injury when the adrenalin is flowing. The problem for Commanche Run in the St Leger was that his mishap hadn't occurred in the race. What he suffered can hit a horse's condition. In the end, he travelled to the races well enough – in general he was fine travelling – and he didn't seem too subdued, so the work in the yard had done the trick, we thought. But he didn't win as easily as we might have liked.'

Lester and Commanche Run were now the team – for ten furlongs. 'We knew that the jockey switch hadn't gone down too well with the boss,' Willows continues. 'I don't remember Lester coming to the yard, but after winning on Commanche Run at Goodwood, ahead of the St Leger, he must have just got on the phone. Commanche Run was owned by Ivan Allan. I guess they knew each other from Hong Kong. With that in mind, the jockey switch wasn't such a surprise. And the switch from St Leger and a mile and three-quarters to shorter trips was no problem for Luca. His horses never gallop more than nine furlongs anyway, so Commanche Run kept his speed all right. Any further than nine furlongs on the gallops at home would be very unusual, and the staying horses would most likely work over just seven furlongs. Commanche Run always had speed. Still, bringing him back so successfully to ten furlongs was a great achievement. He won the Irish Champion Stakes and the old Benson and Hedges in 1985 with Lester riding, and if he'd won the Champion Stakes at Newmarket he'd have won a huge bonus for what they called the ten-furlong Triple Crown. I was in Italy the day of the final leg at Newmarket. I rang up to find out the bad news. We were out of luck that day.

'The Irish Champion Stakes probably meant more to George than a win at Newmarket would have, or even Commanche Run's Classic. Unlike the St Leger, George certainly travelled for the Irish Champion Stakes. A big family gathering at Phoenix Park for the whole Dunwoody clan. After Commanche Run won the crowds went mad. After all, it was Lester again.'

Darrel McHargue hasn't been forgotten, though. 'I still see him around Newmarket,' Willows says. 'He has always been a pretty nice chap. At the time of Commanche Run a lot of people were critical of his style, but he'd never get horses in the wrong place, or at least not very often. People would carp at the way he used his whip, but at the yard we rated him a pretty good jockey, as well as a nice person. You could warm to him and he was a good talker. Lester? We didn't see that much of him. He only occasionally rode work for us. Everyone knew that Lester wasn't the greatest work jockey – always himself for himself. Was Darrel better with the grooms? Not difficult!'

*

Falbrav and Barathea posed a different challenge to Commanche Run. For a start, the pair went much further afield. 'Falbrav was a beast, in both an intimidating as well as an impressive way,' Willows observes. 'Keith Ledington, who looked after him, was bitten, thrown, everything you could imagine. He'd just grin and bear it, soak it up. Eventually he got to know exactly how the horse worked, the way he thought, his likes and dislikes. He was wonderful-looking, a lovely-looking bay. But you would never call Falbrav a nice horse. He was a monster on the gallops and at the yard, and he knew it.

'Funnily enough, travelling he was an absolute delight. When you are flying, you wait for hours. They want you early, then there are delays. "Hurry up and wait" is what they are really saying. Falbrav, he'd just stand there all day – not a murmur. While others would be dripping in sweat, he'd be as still as anything. Just so long as he had his space, you would not get a murmur out of him. The only problem travelling was persuading him to get into the horsebox. For that we had a lunging whip and we'd have to show him we had that, otherwise he could take the piss all day.

'Barathea was more straightforward, but in his travels he wasn't always lucky. In the 1993 Breeders' Cup at Santa Anita, his first crack at the Mile, he had Gary Stevens riding – very experienced around American tracks. Then, in the race, he was nearly knocked out of it completely on the first turn. After that we knew our fate. After the experience of Santa Anita, the guv'nor encouraged the Jockey Club to build a turn to the specifications of American tracks so that runners could be trained round the bends ahead of their races. They acted pretty quickly and constructed a turn on what we all call Lord Derby's private grounds [Lord Derby owned Stanley House before the Maktoums moved in, and the land adjoins the yard]. We all use it, now, ahead of the Breeders' Cup and other races there. Ahead of Churchill

Downs, where Barathea won the Mile in 1994, he was schooled round this, and that's the drill for all our US runners these days as it's Jockey Club land available to everyone. A year after Santa Anita, Barathea was great round the turn. No problems at all. Whether he would have been fine at Churchill Downs without the extra work we'll never know. We just made sure that there was no repeat of Santa Anita. No waste again of a good season and all the effort of preparing a horse.'

'For Barathea's first Breeders' Cup at Santa Anita we went on the charter with the rest of the runners from Europe and flew from Stansted, along with runners like Ezzoud. We were pretty bullish, and when a few travel together there is also a real sense of team. I'd guess it's a bit like the Ryder Cup. In other words, if we don't win, hope you do. A good few went that year to Santa Anita. Whatever people say, the track there is actually not humid, just very dry. That isn't so bad for European horses, so long as the races are in the late afternoon and not any earlier. Florida is the hard one, climate-wise.

'For Churchill Downs, Only Royale also came along with Barathea. We went early, so on our own. This time it was under our own steam, from Stansted to Newark, then Newark down to Louisville, direct. We went on the Fed Ex flight, then changed on to, I think, a DC-8. With just our horses it was like being in a cathedral. The journey had quite a complex change at Newark, and Barathea had also cut his chin on the stall. I had my medicine chest with me –

Americans are fine about that, compared to the Japanese – and we had a torch and could just see the wound. In the circumstances we did our best to clean up the cuts while we were in the air, and after changing planes at Newark we called ahead to ask if a vet could meet us. We eventually arrived in the early morning and the vet who met us was quite happy with the wound. I wasn't so sure, and when we arrived at the track I was even less so. For such situations Luca had given me the details of a local vet, so I called him. Doc Cheney – no relation to Dick in the White House – was a local boy who chewed tobacco and spat all the time. This hillbilly type had a look. "We need a torch," said the lad who looked after Barathea. "Why do you wanna burn down the goddamn barn?" asked Doc Cheney. He was a very highly regarded vet, Cheney. He would have understood "flashlight" better. In the end, Barathea had to have stitches/staples under his chin. You'll notice in the pictures that the other runners we had wore nosebands. We couldn't get one on Barathea.'

Willows was back at Santa Anita nine years later with Falbrav. 'For the Breeders' Cup there with Falbrav, the local box driver tried to bully our boy into the horsebox. He wasn't having any of that. The driver banged his shoulder into him, to nudge him up the ramp. Never try and bully a bully. You'd never hit him with the lunging whip. You wouldn't actually have to, and wouldn't want to either. Just the sound of a crack was enough. Without Keith Ledington we always struggled to get Falbrav into a horsebox. In 2003, when we had to go to Hong Kong for the Hong Kong Cup, he travelled ahead which left us to catch Falbrav and box him up on our own. In the end we had to send for Marco Botti, Luca's assistant, who also rode him a bit. It was nearly midnight, but Marco, who was the son of a trainer, was our plan B without Keith around. We managed to load Falbrav in the end. With him, you didn't push or make a fuss. It was more a case of, "Do you mind, please?"

'In fact, the Hong Kong flight was delayed. It was a jumbo with the horses down below and space for us upstairs. By the time we left we were quite late. During a break, one of the pilots told us that with the delay, China was denying us airspace. So we had to divert to Vietnamese-controlled sky. Time was running out for the pilots to receive permission and the only alternative was to head for Bangkok instead. That would then have meant that the crew had exceeded the air time they are allowed on any one stretch without a break, so we'd have been grounded for a good few hours in the baking heat on the tarmac. Equally, we could have ended up being escorted down by fighter planes for having entered airspace illegally. It was only five to ten minutes before we reached Vietnamese-controlled airspace when we got permission to fly overhead.

'I suppose Falbrav was more the finished article when he arrived at the yard. There was a real sense of expectation. He was a Japan Cup winner, so we knew we had a proven horse. Compared to other horses who have come to the yard – like, say, Starcraft – it was different. When you have a

Japan Cup winner you know they are good compared to the European competition, as there are form lines to consider. With one from somewhere like Australia, or even America, it can be more of an unknown. In the case of Starcraft, who had won the 2004 Australian Derby, we watched videos that showed him run past horses like he was passing lamp-posts. Even so, you really knew more about where you were with the Japan Cup.

'What we managed with Falbrav seemed to leave Luciano Salice, Falbrav's owner, happy enough. Mr Salice speaks a little bit more English than he lets on. A bit like Eric Cantona, I suppose. Salice actually means "Willow" in Italian. He told me that one day, so he must have a bit more of a vocabulary than he let on during Falbrav's success. He could certainly speak enough English to make his point.'

*

Gerald Leigh's Markofdistinction fell short in the 1990 Breeders' Cup, but he flew at Ascot. Likewise the same owner's Gossamer, who saved her very best for Ireland. 'Markofdistinction had a brilliant temperament,' Willows recalls. 'He was a good old stick and also developed physically through his career. He was very dark. You cannot say black because they reckon that's unlucky, but he was as close as you get, and near-black colts always stand out to the eye. We saw plenty of early promise in him. He didn't come from humble beginnings, he was well bred, so we were expecting something. Compared to the other milers we had before him like Second Set and Bairn, I would put him just ahead. Bairn was always a bit fragile for me, quite small.

'I travelled with Markofdistinction to New York for the Breeders' Cup and thought that he would win that day. In the end he just petered out. We also went to America for the Caesars International. That was at Atlantic City. You don't see that very often on At the Races. I've never been so hot in my life – even hotter than Chicago and Tolomeo's Arlington Million. Markofdistinction got bitten to death by flies. All we ever seemed to do in the days before the race was spray him, but it hardly seemed to make a difference.

'He was in much better shape for the Queen Elizabeth II Stakes in 1990. We had two Group One races that day; Shamshir's Fillies' Mile was the other. I think that the races were Frankie's first Group One wins. He'd come a long way from the days when I'd take horses to Milan where I first met him. He hasn't really changed, though. I am Arsenal, and he is still Arsenal – and Juventus. Still remembers where he came from. When he started we would take him racing and kick his backside. Ray [Cochrane], who is now his agent, would give him a really hard time. Frankie would be talking, talking, talking, and Ray would end up saying, "Frankie, please just shut up." His enthusiasm means he's always great to have around.

'Gerald Leigh was such a nice man. He had some good ones with us, including Gossamer. She was a tiny, scruffy thing as a yearling. The majority of Gerald Leigh's were broken in at his farm, and when they arrived at the yard they'd still have long manes. She still turned into a lovely lady. She was always quite small, but wasn't at all delicate. She worked brilliantly, especially on soft ground. There was no hint that she'd like it soft from her movement and the way she walked. The opposite, in fact. A little thing like her should bounce off the fast ground. She had a great temperament for a filly. Most of our good fillies have been quite straightforward, as I remember them. None of our good ones have been much like colts either, which some people say is often a feature of the best fillies. Of Gerald's, only Infamy fits that profile. She was a real hard ride. I didn't get the leg up, thank God.

'You always hope that the smaller ones, those of Gossamer's size, grow from two to three. She didn't, and that was it. Still, she was perfectly put together. After the Guineas here at Newmarket in 2002, when she ran terribly, we were devastated. She ran no sort of race – a real mystery. We were left scratching our heads. But she came good later at the Curragh in the Irish 1,000 Guineas.'

*

For all the problems Willows claims to have when it comes to remembering dates, the fifth of November should stick, notwithstanding the general encouragement that exists to remember (remember) bonfire night. On 5 November 2004 Willows ended up in hospital, lucky to be alive. The horsebox he was driving back to Bedford House from Milan carrying a successful Famcapii was written off when an Italian haulage truck driven by Romanians crunched into the back of him on the hard shoulder at Troyes, east of Paris. Luckily for Willows, he was checking the engine at the time – the radiator had overheated and could only be accessed from the side – otherwise he'd have needed more than just an overnight stop in hospital to deal with cuts to his head, which left a scar, and a stiff neck, which was still the worse for whiplash six months on. Famcapii and travelling companion Terenzium were both loose on the motorway. The former had suffered bad injuries and was humanely destroyed.

Such occurrences make you savour all the more great moments such as Barathea gave Willows. 'He was a lovely horse,' he says. 'Winning the Breeders' Cup was a big thrill. I don't like to say Barathea is my favourite – there have been plenty to choose from in that respect. But he was always lovely to look at, even as a yearling. The good ones don't always stand out. Gossamer looked awful, remember. We said, "What's that?" But Barathea was always striking. One to keep your eye on, for sure. From his arrival, he grew and blossomed. You might get a germ of a thought that you have a Classic winner on your hands through August and September. With Barathea, going into the winter of 1993 I thought he was the best chance we had of winning the Guineas. Compared to Bairn, who was second to Shadeed, he certainly stood out as having better prospects. He was never a weed or anything like that. From three to four he certainly filled out. Being away, you see them change.

Mentally, too. In his case, at two he was pretty sensible; then he just got more and more experienced. When Churchill Downs came round, he was ready.'

Just over three weeks after Willows's stay at the hands of French medical care he volunteered to return to hospital in relatively happier circumstances. On 29 November he finally had a long-awaited hip replacement to alleviate the consequences of a fracture two decades earlier that had left one leg three-quarters of an inch shorter than the other. He's fit now for the golf he expects to play long into his retirement. Having helped Commanche Run to register a special place in history, he might reasonably expect a few strokes' advantage and some generosity on the green if paired with Lester Piggott. 'Saw him swing a club recently,' Willows confides. 'Never seen him play before then.'

CHAPTER TEN
RODNEY BOULT

Over 50 years in racing,
mornings with Dessie and Punch

Horses were a remote thought for Rodney Boult back in Liverpool after the Second World War. Then, snooker held his attention. At five stone nothing, and without any reason to duck, he stood on a box to see off all-comers at the table in his family's leisure club. Locals, fed up with losing, had the idea that he should quit hustling and become a jockey instead.

Today, after over 50 years in racing, Boult probably owes them a debt of gratitude for their wise counsel. Likewise to David Elsworth. To begin with he was best man at Boult's wedding to Shirley. Then, two decades later, Elsworth, at his Whitsbury stables, offered Boult the chance to share in perhaps British racing's greatest ever story. When Elsworth invited Boult to climb into the saddle of Desert Orchid, whom he so brilliantly trained, the veteran work rider, these days well past retirement age, became part of legend.

Long before then, first stop for Boult was Newmarket

and Marcus Marsh. The Aga Khan of the day, one of only five owners at the yard, would come to see his Derby winner Tulyar. Being around the season's best in 1952 – Tulyar also won the King George at Ascot, the Eclipse and the St Leger – was a good start for Boult's confidence. Charlie Smirke, the stable jockey never short of cockney belief, also boosted self-esteem levels. Terry Spinks was part of the team too, before he gained Olympic gold at boxing in 1956.

Without much chance of a ride, Boult next headed for Major Fred Sneyd's yard. Joe Mercer, on his way to riding for the Queen, was good company. There were also chickens to feed when the gardener wasn't around. Then came Doug Marks' yard – plenty of competition there for the best morning ride. The hopefuls included David Elsworth.

It all might have been different had Boult stayed out of the game after yet another hard winter in 1961. He went back to club life, this time in the family's new place in Wales. After six years it was Joe Mercer who hauled him back into racing. Boult had given up on becoming a jockey, but Mercer said he would still get to ride out at Dick Hern's West Ilsley yard. There was plenty more action in the saddle, and a house, when Boult moved on once again to Lord Astor's stable. Likewise when his travels took him to John Dunlop and Arundel. There, Boult really got started again. With Shirley Heights, he filled another Derby winner's saddle. 'Lazy bones', as Boult called him, also went on to win in Ireland.

Boult couldn't have known what was still to come. Who

could? Perhaps only Elsworth could have had an inkling. With hindsight, Whitsbury was inevitably Boult's ultimate destination once Elsworth had made camp. As for Dessie, before Boult he'd had his fair share of partners, but after a difficult first season he only ever had the one work rider. For Boult, there were other memorable partnerships, making the most of Elsworth's prowess on the Flat. In The Groove was nurtured by Boult to a Classic win, the 1,000 Guineas, in Ireland (incidentally, Boult's daughter Simone featured in her saddle as well). Another filly, Dead Certain, gave him the thrill of shaping a career that featured Group One and Royal Ascot successes. Other leading lights over the jumps were Barnbrook Again, twice a Queen Mother Champion Chase winner (1989 and the following year), and Oh So Risky, Triumph Hurdle hero and Cheltenham Festival veteran. On the Flat there was Naheez, second to Sir Harry Lewis in the 1987 Irish Derby, and Indian Ridge. As for other celebrities, Persian Punch was as close to a Dessie as the summer game gets. 'Punch' was tragically taken from racing by, of all things, a weak heart. For Boult, the memory of the gelding's collapse at Ascot in April 2004 ranks with the day a decade or so earlier when Seattle Rhyme, a Group One colt like Naheez and Indian Ridge, was also claimed by the game on the Whitsbury gallops.

So, performers of the highest rank for most summers and plenty of success at the winter game, in addition to Dessie. For Boult, it doesn't begin and end with the grey. But that is where everyone usually wants to start.

*

'Desert Orchid was so smooth,' says Boult. 'The action, the feel, the balance, the flow of a good horse. You cover the ground as if you are gliding. Dessie? Always fresh as a new two-year-old, legs included. Without a mark even today. His action was perfect. He never had a scratch on him from the day he arrived at Whitsbury to the day he left. One day a groom put bandages on him. "What have you done that for?" I asked. "We always put boots on them," he said. He didn't need them on the gallops. Maybe boots for schooling and racing, like all jumpers, but never, ever on the gallops.

'If jumpers are not broken in until late, a lot of three- and four-year-olds can find it a bit of a shock. They have had a holiday for three years, then they have to graft. They worry. Dessie did, especially. When he arrived he wasn't eating and he was pulling. Looked terrible. I saw him one day across the gallops. Afterwards, I asked, "Who is that pulling?" He was sweating, head in the air, looked horrible. That was his first year. He had one run, then went home. When he came back, I'd been at the yard for a good few months. By then it felt like I belonged. When Dessie ducked out and dropped his rider one morning, Elzzie – that's what I've always called David Elsworth – asked me to have a go. He pulled for sure, so I just took extra precautions to hold him. It is one thing to settle a horse, but you have to hold them first. After that it's a case of sitting quiet, talking to the horse, giving them some confidence. In the main, the horse is worried, and most horses don't have the biggest brains in the world.

If they think you are going to work them hard, they'll think, "This is going to be tough." You have to let them know that there's nothing to worry about. Takes days and days. But if you do it right, those days will get better and better and better. Pull them around, you affect the brain. "Oi, my mouth's a bit sore – leave it out," they'll be thinking.

'We made sure Dessie enjoyed a regular pattern of work and feed. All of a sudden, after a year, he started to eat up. Was he pulling so hard? No. Was he sweating so much? No. Was he stronger looking? Yes. Did he put on weight? Yes. And more relaxed. To start with, going to the canter he would be dancing with worry a hundred yards or so from the start. By the end of that season he was still dancing but just for the two or three strides before we kicked off. A few steps, then we'd be away. Someone once said to me, "Rodney, you shouldn't be dancing at all, you should walk all the way to the gallops." I thought, "Let's just get him there. Dance if you like. Meantime, we'll keep ourselves to ourselves and have a chat."'

Barnbrook Again was good company too. 'We'd work with Barney. Ross Arnott rode him. They would always work with Desert Orchid, as Dessie was capable of making the running. He was actually a very good one to make the pace for Barnbrook to follow as we would go a mile, a mile and a quarter, a mile and a half, and Ross would have a great blow. Mind you, he would have to say, "I'll settle for finishing two lengths behind you." Even before his Queen Mother wins when Barnbrook was at the top of his game,

Barnbrook didn't head Dessie. No one could. Even good jumpers like Hypnosis, Rhyme 'N' Reason. We would finish at the top of the hill and I'd always be left on my own.

'Barney was always very good-natured. A gem compared to the likes of, say, Oh So Risky. We didn't see Barney unbroken. He came to us after that from Ireland. He was always a good, well-proportioned horse, a lovely jumper. He'd really ping his fences, as he was a natural. We never needed to school him much. Everything was easy for him. Throughout his career we never had any scares in the weeks before his big races. Oh So Risky was a much tougher proposition. He'd always anticipate the gallop. As soon as he was at the start, he'd leap off the ground, over and over, and on the way to the gallops as well. He'd cut the corners on the way too. In all, quite a handful.' Horses can be like that.

'If it's a case of your brain against one of their brains, you should be fine,' Boult continues. 'Dessie could always worry. I used to say anything to him, even sing, just to make him listen. If he can't hear me, he might think, "We are going to have to go flat out, he's going to yank me about soon, and it'll be horrible." So I'd whisper in his ear, "Whoa der boy, whoa der boy, whoa d'boy.' He'd be pulling and I'd be straining, saying "Whoa d'boy" all the time. Plus I'd be sitting still in the right part of the saddle for holding. That's not back in the saddle because you won't be able to give a bit. You should be upright and holding, straining every muscle, but just holding. In the end, we got there.'

*

Before Desert Orchid there was Shirley Heights, the 1978 Derby winner Boult rates as his first real contact with star quality. With Dessie to come, he experienced the challenges presented by the very best. 'Shirley Heights always ate well,' Boult recalls. 'The guv'nor gave him a rest after the Irish Derby. Within a few weeks he was like a broodmare. He never got light, even after he won at Epsom. My wife – she's called Shirley too – gave him some flowers after the Derby. There was a picture in the paper of them in his box. He ate them.

'I remember the moment, months before Epsom, when John Dunlop said Shirley Heights was his Derby horse. He didn't say he might be, but that he was, for sure. I backed him there and then at 33–1. Mack, the local chemist, liked a bet. All the old girls who wouldn't go into the betting shop would ask him to put the money on for them. After the Derby, the bookies had to close three times before everyone in the town was paid.

'Before that, we had to keep Shirley Heights on the road to Epsom. Obviously he was good. His temperament? Another matter altogether. A very, very difficult horse to ride. He had a really small mouth, quite narrow. This meant that he didn't take the bit very well. He'd fiddle away with it as with a mouth like that nothing ever fits. Maybe his mouth might have been messed up when he was a yearling. He also had a spooky eye, so he was always looking for mischief. He'd see things before you, and that would be it.

You'd be riding and he'd think, "There's a dog there," or something unusual. He'd just whip round on you. You'd think, "Where did that come from?"

'You might think it's quite exciting to be with a horse like that, but it isn't always. It's never nice to find yourself always thinking, "Hope I don't do anything silly today." The sweat is that the horse will hurt himself. Falling off is no problem. You get up again. The worry is that the horse will maybe cut his leg. You'd say, "Stupid bloody horse." But you would have been the one in the saddle. Before the Derby, he whipped round on the road when I was with the guv'nor. Shirley Heights fell over and took some skin off his knees. Luckily he didn't suffer anything more serious than that. Other times he would be picking at some grass and then just spin round. Once he took me round three times. I just hung on. Nothing seemed to be moving but he saw something to spook him and that was that. Once he was just picking with some other horses and one jumped towards him so he whipped round again and dropped me. He'd already won the Dante so I was on our Derby horse. You can imagine the anxiety that sort of thing generated.

'Another time before the Derby there had been a lot of rain for a few days. Water had run down the ash track, which was for walking, and had created a channel where the water ran from one side of the track to the other. Just past this mini ditch there was a conker tree that hung a bit low. That was where he spooked. He stepped over the gully but still fell over. I had to let him go while he fell but then made sure that I grabbed him as he got up. You couldn't have had him running down through the town. Arundel is not like Newmarket. Most people in Arundel don't know what to do with horses. Who knows what could have happened? John Dunlop reckoned that Shirley Heights took years off my life. A real firecracker.'

Shirley Heights' trainer never turned a hair, even ahead of the Curragh. 'The guv'nor somehow never seemed worried,' Boult recalls. 'John Dunlop was – is – always laid back. In the spring, before Epsom, the cameras were at the yard to film Shirley Heights in a gallop. We also had a horse called North Stoke, a really good one the guv'nor trained to win six races on the bounce in five different countries – Ireland, Belgium, England, Scotland and Germany. The lad riding him jumped off after the work as he had pulled up lame. Even though this was being filmed, John Dunlop didn't panic. You get this, you get the bandages, you go back to the yard and fetch the box.

'I was worried before the Irish Derby. Shirley Heights certainly wasn't a bad worker. At worst, he was slightly lazy. But his last gallop before the Irish Derby certainly looked bad. At the start of the all-weather gallops his lead horse took a couple of slaps so he would kick on and give Shirley Heights something to aim at, but I was actually left four lengths and I never got to him. Shirley seemed to think, "I'm not close enough to catch him." There were four days to go before the race and things weren't looking great. The guv'nor flew the horse early to the Curragh and we worked again the day before the race. We galloped up a peat moss gallop – the stuff was bulging out of the ground, whereas here we can't afford the stuff – and there wasn't a soul on hand to watch. The lead horse was a good horse. Shirley Heights still absolutely flew six furlongs. I could hardly pull him up.

'In general, we had to gallop him every Sunday as he was such a man of a horse. He was always so fresh; you wouldn't want him all wound up for Monday morning. This way, we tried to keep him calmer. You can't really calm a horse like that. I always carried a stick but only ever gave him the one slap after he slipped on the road and ran back to the yard. I thought then that he was taking the mickey out of me, so I gave him a crack. The guv'nor said, "Don't hit him, Rodney." "But we have to tell him that he's not allowed to do that," I said. He needed to know that if I say go that way, that is the way we go.

'The Curragh gallop was a last resort. Sometimes a change of scenery can work like that. The guv'nor always tried to freshen up the good ones with a trip away a week or so before their big races. With Shirley Heights, we'd actually go to Pulborough. The alternative was to the gallops at Lady Herries' place. There was a twelve-furlong stretch through the valley there, with the last four furlongs finishing up a hill which would really set them right for what was ahead. At Arundel we had a mile stretch, but we had to pull up after about six furlongs as there was just wide-open space after the mile. If we galloped beyond that we might not be able to stop them. My wife and I would walk up those gallops thinking that there might be a stone or two we should find, just in case there were any that could affect Shirley Heights. Me, Shirley, the kids and dogs. Magical days.'

*

Tulyar preceded Shirley Heights and represented a contrast. A rookie Rodney Boult had a taste of the Derby big time, and Charlie Smirke, and learnt not to underestimate talent. 'Compared to Shirley Heights, Tulyar was an insignificant little horse,' he says. 'Sometimes homebreds in those days could be a bit wild, but he came from a money stud. He was well behaved from day one. Where he came from – he was bred by the Aga Khan – there were always enough staff around to take him in hand. To be honest, I was a bit underwhelmed by Tulyar at first. The reason he left you a bit flat was that he always stumbled coming home from the gallops. I'd say now that was because he couldn't be bothered to walk. You see the same in good footballers. They walk along with their shoulders hunched. But when you see them on the pitch, everything is different.

'In Newmarket in the early 1950s I was single and just getting into racing. At Marcus Marsh's yard with Tulyar it was different to Arundel and Shirley Heights. I was only learning about the game. When we got this two-year-old, as I said, I didn't think much of him. He got beaten, got beaten, got beaten, got beaten. Nothing special to me at the time. Why would he be? For all I knew!' Nursery success under steadying weights prompted Boult to reconsider. 'He won at Haydock and, in those days, Birmingham. I thought, "Maybe we have got a racehorse here." With hindsight, and a few years' experience, I think that he was just a slow developer. Even at three he wasn't very big and was still stumbling everywhere. He didn't show a lot on the gallops either. His temperament was great, though. A very switched-off colt. He was quite a tough ride in the winter. Marsh had to put up one of the best on him, as he was always a bit fresh. But most good athletes are like that when they are working. After the 1952 Derby, we won the Eclipse, the King George and then the St Leger. Looking back, I think he would have won the Guineas too if he had been given the chance to run. There was always something left.

'He missed Newmarket as he didn't show that much speed. The Aga Khan, who owned him, and Marcus Marsh decided to keep him for the Derby and skip running in the 2,000 Guineas at Newmarket. The ground was also firm, which he was supposed to dislike. He ran good trials – won at Hurst Park, Chester and Lingfield. Then the ground came up fast at Epsom. They decided to take a chance and run anyway. Charlie Smirke just won. Lester Piggott rode the second, Gay Time. After the Derby, he was going around saying, "We'll beat him in the King George. I'd have won the Derby if I hadn't spread a plate." Charlie just smiled. "OK, Lester," he said, "we'll see." In the King George he won again – cheeky. Broke Gay Time's heart in the process. Charlie had been at the Derby dinner the week of Epsom and told everyone, "I'll win." The horse was 14–1 at the time but shorter on the day. Charlie was a cocky cockney, with a big old mouth. After the race he was telling everyone, "I told you so, didn't I? Didn't I Tulyar!" We had a party in the big hotel at Newmarket. After three halves of lager I was drunk. A free bar for the whole stable. It didn't really matter that I was new to the game. We won the Derby! Great times.

'If the Aga Khan visited the yard, I had to cover the passages with white sawdust to make the place as smart as a butcher's shop. He'd walk along the boxes looking at the horses. "This one belongs to you," the guv'nor would say. "So does this one, and this one as well." The Aga's son Aly Khan would sometimes come too, with Rita Hayworth on his arm. She always looked fantastic, even though she wasn't made up for filming. In those days, women like her just didn't dress casual.'

*

Naheez went close to emulating Shirley Heights in the 1987 Irish Derby. In the Groove went one better at the Curragh three years later. All the while she was starring at the racetrack, she had company at home in Dead Certain. The latter's summer peak was the year before at Royal Ascot, in the 1989 Queen Mary Stakes.

'Naheez was a good horse,' Boult says. 'He was like a six-foot schoolboy who always stays slim, tall and leggy. As a two-year-old early on he only managed soft work. He didn't have the muscle for much else. But he already had the action. We thought, "We've got one here." But it took him time to develop the strength. He was never going to be a giant but he was always going to be good. You look at some juveniles and think, "Too big, too tall, too leggy." But he could gallop straight away. He had a great action when he was moving, even walking. Good enough, ultimately, to win the Horris Hill as a two-year-old.

'At three, you could see that he was getting stronger. In the end, his strength almost frightened me. In the spring, the guv'nor asked me to go a mile and a half on him round this loop we have at Whitsbury. They can pull a bit round there as the ground goes up and down, so I had to settle in behind a couple who Elzzie said would increase the tempo as we made our way round. At the start I got left ten lengths, so I made the ground up as slowly as I could. With five furlongs still to go, all uphill, I caught up with them, which I thought was perfect. "He settled nicely in the end," I told the guv'nor. "But you gave them a furlong start," he said. If I hadn't, I knew I would not have been able to keep behind them down the hill. He moved so well. For all the power, though, he couldn't quite quicken. If he'd had that ability he'd have won the Irish Derby. Sir Harry Lewis, who did win, had first run on him. After that they both carried on at the same pace. If we'd had first run, the result would have been reversed. Then he got a leg.

'I expected less of In The Groove. I remember her first day in the yard. The guv'nor came over to me. "Bought that, Rod," he said. "But guv'nor, she looks like a broodmare!"

She had short legs and her belly was on the floor. I would not have been a fan at first. A plain Jane with a belly. Certainly nothing to write home about. But during the winter, from two to three, she got rid of her belly. She also grew. Come the spring she was very powerful with a real backside full of power. As well as growing up she grew out, which meant that she was quite masculine to look at. We had a horse. You can see them blossom. You don't even need to go away to notice the changes. You can just stand back and say, "She has grown. She's come along, at least an inch." Sometimes they do go backwards, but she didn't. She was usually quite laid back but could be lively and would sometimes have her moments and her moans. She'd whip round, and going into a canter she could drop you. Just high spirits.

'She began to shift at two after Royal Ascot. My daughter, Simone, was the yard's secretary at the time, and was an amateur rider in her own right. We were all going to gallop one morning. I was on Dead Certain, who had won the Queen Mary, and Simone was on In The Groove, who had been beaten in a maiden. Halfway up the hill I thought, "Blimey, she's going as well as me." So I tried to get a bit more out of Dead Certain, and more, and more. But whatever I tried I couldn't get to the front. Afterwards I said to the guv'nor that I was worried Dead Certain was working really lazy. "No she isn't," he said. "That filly I bought, she's bloody good." He wasn't joking all right. I think he saw ability in her from the way she walked. She also had a good old-fashioned character and real build about her.

'She was beaten as a three-year-old only because no one knew how to ride her. At Newmarket in 1990 in the 1,000 Guineas we fancied her and she bolted off in front, but then emptied. Then we worked out that she needed to be held up. It was different at the Curragh. We had to try something else as we had all this horse travelling and she wasn't finishing. At halfway in all her races you'd say we were going to win. Come the Champion Stakes at the end of her three-year-old season, she was awesome. She didn't really get a mile and a half, which is why she was beaten in the Oaks. She did win the Coronation Cup at Epsom as a four-year-old, but that was an easy twelve furlongs that day.'

Dead Certain was different to In The Groove. 'Good from day one,' says Boult. 'I don't normally like to brag about the rides, but we had photographers down in the spring so I said, "Take one of Dead Certain – she's going to be good." Then she was beaten first time out, in May 1989 at Windsor. She got the hang of it next time at Salisbury. It wasn't a worry when she didn't win her maiden. She took Royal Ascot in her stride easily enough. She came back to the yard and you wouldn't know that she had had a race.

'The girls rode her to start with, but one or two of them were struggling on her so the guv'nor called me in for her, a bit like he did with Dessie. She wasn't a bad size at all, and she was on her toes. We got on well straight away. My daughter said she found her a bit tricky, but I always found her fine. She was good and tough, like all good horses. If they were duck-hearted, then forget it. They can take their racing. She did hate the mud being kicked back in her face, though. When that happened she tried to duck it and slow down. Her head would go back. Luckily, on the gallops at home there was never any serious kickback. Apart from mud, she was never a madam. She never got loose or anything like that. When she was flat out she was very smooth, like a fast car. Suddenly you'd be away with her.'

*

The warmth and depth in Boult's voice when he talks about Desert Orchid is also present for Persian Punch. 'He was a big, gangly horse,' Boult recalls. 'I didn't ride him in the early days, but I could still see that he covered so much ground because he was seventeen hands. As a young horse he was very unfurnished, but an athlete's an athlete. At the same time, always a lovely character. Punch was always very nice, and friendly. You'd say hello to him. He was one of those horses who liked company and had a huge heart. Without that, you simply don't win the races he won. All the good ones have the heart. They eat a healthy meal so that they are ready for racing and the prospect doesn't worry them. And when it's a hard race, they shrug it off.'

'He ran for the first time at Windsor in May 1996. Anthony Procter rode him. At the races, he asked me, "Can you lengthen with him?" "Oh yes, you can," I said. He won at 20–1. We hadn't galloped him hard so we didn't know for sure how good he might be. We did know that he would get better as he got older. The hope was that by the time he was four he would catch up with his frame. In the meantime, he was fine. If you have ability, you can tie up a leg and you've still got the ability. At six, people began to say that he couldn't improve any more. But he was being ridden forcefully, from the front. At this point we decided to make it just a staying gallop. Don't knock him about to make sure the gallop is a scorcher. Just keep asking, like Martin Dwyer always did. Then the improvement came.'

The work at home was sometimes hard. 'On the gallops we'd make it a graft, but not so hard that he'd lose interest,' Boult continues. 'He'd go halfway up the hill and you'd feel him beneath you saying, "That's enough, no more." So you'd ask him again. He'd say, "OK then, just a bit more." He had speed all right. He'd be asked to work with the sprinters to give him a little glow, and that big old stride of his meant he was only a couple of lengths off them at the end. They would take the upper hand, but only in the last furlong. With his competitive spirit he would want to take them on and at least stay with them. Plus, to win the Gold Cup you need to travel. The Derby winner is travelling like a sprinter when he takes charge of the race even though they run a mile and a half. Speed is essential to win any horse race.

'The guv'nor kept him fresh. Every night he would put a headcollar on him and lead him up the hill. He'd let him roll around a bit in the sandpit, and pick some grass. Just for twenty minutes on his own, to make him feel special. The old horse loved it.

'The way Persian Punch died, at Ascot in front of the

stands, was so lousy. That shouldn't happen to such a big-hearted horse. Seattle Rhyme, who won the Racing Post Trophy in 1991, was worse for me. I was riding him at home on the gallops when he broke his leg and I ended up holding him. That was hard to turn your back on. But I wasn't at Ascot for Punch. If I had been there, getting over it would have been much, much harder.'

*

To the racing community, Rodney Boult is inseparable from Persian Punch and, in particular, Desert Orchid. Also from David Elsworth. 'Elzzie's never too hard on them as two-year-olds at home,' Boult says, 'and at the races he makes sure jockeys take care of them. That's even if he has had £1,000 to win. I have seen him have a good bet on a horse, then tell the jockey, "Don't you knock him about now." He thinks about the horse, never the bet. I've also heard him say, "This one's a bit nervous. He needs to be nice and quiet at the back. And don't touch him if you think it might set him back at all. I want him to come home, and to have enjoyed it." Then he'll have £50 to win.

'At Whitsbury, we don't ride out with sticks and there are no stalls on the gallops. We're not like some trainers who spend every day teaching them to jump out. For ours, their first day at the races is like, "Oh, where am I? Oh, I see." That way they are always better next time and you reap the benefits later on because they improve. The guv'nor always works the two-year-olds together at first, over the same trip.

That way they tell you what is what. You look at them and see the changes – ones who have come up a bit light, ones who have gone backwards, the ones developing along the lines you hope. Before Ascot you might give them a bit more of a challenge on the gallops, maybe work with the three-year-olds, as you need to find out if they are good enough.'

Indian Ridge was a case in point. 'He won the Jersey Stakes in 1988 and the King's Stand Stakes, also at Royal Ascot, the following year,' Boult recalls. 'He was a natural. Very good and very tough. His first day on the gallops, he powered up the middle and finished a neck in front of the pack – two double handfuls of reins. We could only hope. At the time, we hadn't had a two-year-old runner. We couldn't be sure how good he was. Then we had our first two-year-old of the season and he ran well. So we thought, "We've a good one here." Then he got beat on his debut. We went to Salisbury for his first run. I thought, "We'll win all right." But there was something running around like a mad thing in the paddock – a big, black, randy colt. We were beaten by five lengths. It was Warning. So two Group One horses in the same race. It can happen. There wasn't much in it between Indian Ridge and Dead Certain. He was usually on his toes, but not always, which is the case for some sprinters. Even when he was close to a race, he didn't get geed up. You could still hack-canter with him and he always took his races well. Sometimes the good ones are very straightforward.'

Elzzie usually works them out. 'With horses, David Elsworth is uncanny,' Boult reckons. 'It's the only word to describe him – uncanny. Pretty uncanny in every respect, really. Seems to read your mind. He'll appear round a corner. "Knew you'd be here doing that," he'll say. He is on to you because he has sensed that you might end up doing something wrong. Keeps you on your toes. A true master of horses. With people? A hard taskmaster, that's for sure. I always believe in a dressing down when it's deserved and credit when you've done well. He's not really that way. We could go into a box where the groom had done a great job and he would say nothing. I'd say, "Well done, the horse looks a picture," and be set to leave. At which point he'd stop and point out how something could have been done differently.'

Sometimes, a little bit of John Dunlop can be better for morale. 'On the day of Shirley Heights' Derby there was a PR tent outside the castle,' Boult recalls. 'There must have been some function taking place. Before the race, we lifted up the bottom of the tent and shouted through, "How about some champagne if Shirley Heights wins the Derby?" After he did, I was walking past the tent again and someone shouted out, "Here you are!" and shoved two bottles into my hands. I found some nice plastic cups and went back to the yard. When I saw the guv'nor, I asked him, "Shall we open these?" "Where did you get those from?" he asked. "On second thoughts," he added, "none of my business!"'

INDEX

INDEX